Libya's Displacement Crisis

Uprooted by Revolution and Civil War

Related Titles

The African Renaissance and the Afro-Arab Spring: A Season of Rebirth?
edited by Charles Villa-Vicencio, Erik Doxtader, and Ebrahim Moosa

Driven from Home: Protecting the Rights of Forced Migrants
edited by David Hollenbach, SJ

Tunisian Revolutions: Reflections on Seas, Coasts, and Interiors
by Julia Clancy-Smith

Libya's Displacement Crisis
Uprooted by Revolution and Civil War

Megan Bradley, Ibrahim Fraihat, and Houda Mzioudet

GEORGETOWN UNIVERSITY PRESS

© 2016 Georgetown University Press. All rights reserved. No part of this book may be reproduced or utilized in any form or by any means, electronic or mechanical, including photocopying and recording, or by any information storage and retrieval system, without permission in writing from the publisher.

Join our mailing list and get updates on new releases and special offers from Georgetown University Press.

Library of Congress Cataloging-in-Publication Data

Bradley, Megan, 1980- author.
   Libya's displacement crisis : uprooted by revolution and civil war / Megan Bradley, Ibrahim Fraihat, and Houda Mzioudet.
      pages   cm
   Includes bibliographical references and index.
   ISBN 978-1-62616-329-4 (pbk. : alk. paper) -- ISBN 978-1-62616-330-0 (ebook)
   1. Refugees—Libya.2. Libya—History—Civil War, 2011—Refugees. I. Fraihat, Ibrahim, author II. Mzioudet, Houda, author III. Title.
   HV640.5.L48B73 2016
   961.205—dc23   2015034373

∞ This book is printed on acid-free paper meeting the requirements of the American National Standard for Permanence in Paper for Printed Library Materials.

17 16   9 8 7 6 5 4 3 2   First printing

Printed in the United States of America

Cover design by Pam Pease
Cover image by Dominique Faget / AFP / Getty Images

Contents

Acknowledgments vii

Introduction ix
   Conceptual Issues xii

Chronology xvii

1. Background: A Fallen Regime, Victor's Justice, and Resurgent Violence 1
   The Fall of the Gaddafi Regime 1
   The Rise of Victor's Justice 2
   The Initial Displacement Crisis 6
   Civil War and the Reescalation of the Displacement Crisis 8

2. A Growing Crisis: Internal Displacement in Post-Gaddafi Libya 16
   A "Constant Nightmare": Daily Life and Protection Challenges for Libyan IDPs 17
   Lackluster Responses and Barriers to Solutions 20

3. Precarious Refuge: Displaced Libyans in North Africa 29
   Into the Shadows: Libyans' Search for Invisibility in Neighboring Countries 30

Insecure Status, Lack of Documentation, and Fear of Return	33
Declining Living Conditions	37
Dismantling an "Army of Opposition," Advancing Durable Solutions	40
4. Durable Solutions: Obstacles and Prospects	52
The Lynchpin: Security and Rule of Law	53
Participation in Dialogues and Negotiations	54
Transitional Justice, Reconciliation, and the Resolution of Displacement	55
Conclusions and Recommendations	58
Shorter-Term Recommendations	58
Longer-Term Recommendations (Relevant for a Postconflict Context)	60
About the Authors	62

Acknowledgments

WE WOULD LIKE to thank all those who supported the completion of this study, including colleagues with the Foreign Policy Program at the Brookings Institution, the Brookings Doha Center, Tunisians and Libyans who shared their perspectives, and others who supported the logistics of the field research in both Libya and Tunisia. We would also like to express our appreciation for the support of the Brookings Institution Foreign Policy Director's Strategic Initiative Fund.

Introduction

LIBYANS ARE NO STRANGERS to displacement and dispossession. Muammar Gaddafi's forty-two-year rule was marked by the flight of thousands of Libyans into exile, the appropriation of opponents' homes and lands, and the manipulation of relations between tribes, leading to property disputes and sometimes violent conflicts. Yet, the scale of the displacement crisis engendered by the country's 2011 revolution was unprecedented: Out of a population of 6.2 million, 550,000 people were uprooted within the country, while approximately 660,000 sought shelter in neighboring countries, alongside some 670,000 migrants who had been working in Libya before fleeing the erupting conflict.[1] Through a combination of timely humanitarian interventions and the ability of displaced Libyans to draw on their own social and financial resources, the lion's share of the crisis was swiftly resolved, with the majority returning to their homes after the fall of the Gaddafi regime.

However, several complex displacement situations have persisted within Libya while new forced migration crises have emerged. The surge in violence during the summer of 2014 led to what Tarek Mitri, the former special representative of the United Nations (UN) secretary-general for Libya, termed another "unprecedented movement of population," with at least a hundred thousand more people internally displaced by the fighting.[2] By March 2015, with the rise of civil war in Libya, estimates of those internally displaced had risen to four hundred thousand.[3] At the same time, scores more Libyans and migrant workers fled the country, joining the hundreds of thousands of Libyans who have been in exile in neighboring countries for much longer periods, without formal status and often in increasingly dire circumstances.[4] Libyans have not, for the most part, attempted to flee across the Mediterranean to Europe by boat. However, human smugglers have capitalized on the chaos in Libya by expanding their operations, sending increased numbers of asylum seekers and migrants—transiting through Libya primarily from Syria and African states—to Europe in overcrowded, unsafe vessels, leading to thousands of deaths.[5] Although there is significant diversity among those who have been uprooted, many among the more long-standing displaced population are assumed to have been supporters or beneficiaries of the Gaddafi regime. Most were not complicit in human rights abuses, but these exiles nonetheless live in fear of being forcibly returned to Libya, where, in the absence of security, rule of law, and a functional transitional justice process, they may face incarceration, torture, and death.

The continued displacement of Libyan citizens within and outside their country has significant political, socioeconomic, humanitarian, and human rights implications, not only for the displaced themselves, but also for the Libyan state, its neighbors, and the international community. The aim of this book is to analyze the complex dimensions and implications of the Libyan displacement situation. While the resolution of this humanitarian crisis hinges on a negotiated end to the Libyan Civil War, it seeks to help lay the groundwork for this process by identifying constructive strategies to improve present assistance strategies and eventually to support durable solutions for Libyan internally displaced persons (IDPs) and exiles. Although there are sizable Libyan exile populations in several states, we focus in particular on those in Tunisia, where the greatest number of displaced Libyans are sheltered. More than four years after the collapse of the Gaddafi regime, these displacement situations are above all a reflection of the failure to establish security and political stability in postrevolution Libya and to initiate even-handed transitional justice processes that address unresolved grievances and effectively support the broader pursuit of reconciliation among individuals, tribes, and communities and with the state. Supporting durable solutions for displaced Libyans is a critical element of human rights protection in post-Gaddafi Libya and an essential investment in national and regional security, as prolonged displacement risks creating a marginalized population without access to peaceful channels to resolve grievances.

In addition to establishing security and strengthening Libya's enfeebled judiciary, resolving Libya's displacement crises will require the active engagement of uprooted Libyans in revived transitional justice and reconciliation processes. These processes must focus on individual rather than communal responsibility for atrocities—particularly as the overwhelming majority of IDPs and those in exile did not actively participate in human rights violations. They will need to strike an elusive balance between upholding accountability for past violations and avoiding the perception of "victor's justice." This will require that transitional justice and reconciliation efforts address crimes committed not only during the Gaddafi regime, but also in the course of the revolution and the subsequent civil war. Such an undertaking is complicated not only by the fracturing of the Libyan state in the context of the present civil war and the lack of state capacity to enforce law and order, but also by Libya's legal framework, which includes laws that immunize from prosecution those who may have committed war crimes or human rights violations if these acts were "made necessary" by the 17 February Revolution.[6] In Libya and its neighboring states, strengthened policy frameworks and support for their effective implementation are needed to ensure systematic, rights-based responses to both internal and cross-border displacement, building on the incorporation of the right to seek asylum and the prohibition of the extradition of "political refugees" in the new Tunisian constitution. Until the security conditions in Libya stabilize, increased international engagement and support is needed to ensure that Libya's neighbors keep their borders open and can continue to shelter new arrivals.

This book begins by providing a brief background to the displacement crises that emerged in the context of the Libyan Revolution, highlighting the factors that enabled the comparatively prompt resolution of the bulk of the initial crisis but entrenched the displacement of a subset of the uprooted population. It also discusses the displacement patterns that have emerged with the outbreak of civil war. It then engages in a detailed analysis of the political, socioeconomic, security, and humanitarian dimensions of Libya's internal and cross-border displacement situations, focusing in particular on those populations whose displacement is now becoming protracted. This is followed by a discussion of obstacles to durable solutions for displaced Libyans and prospects for addressing these obstacles, with particular emphasis on the relationship between transitional justice and reconciliation processes and the resolution of displacement. This discussion is premised on the recognition that increased security and stability in Libya is the sine qua non for the sustainable resolution of the displacement situation. The book concludes with recommendations for different actors.

The book is based on analysis of relevant laws and policy frameworks, as well as a series of semistructured interviews conducted in 2013 and 2014 (primarily in Libya and Tunisia) with key actors, including current and former representatives of the Libyan and Tunisian governments, international organizations, and civil society groups, members of different IDP communities, and Libyan exiles with varying degrees of involvement with the former regime. The majority of the interviews were undertaken in Arabic and translated into English by the authors. Identifying details have been removed to preserve the confidentiality of displaced interviewees.

Conceptual Issues

Following the 1998 Guiding Principles on Internal Displacement, the term IDP is used in this study to denote those who have been "forced or obliged to flee or to leave their homes or places of habitual residence, in particular as a result of or in order to avoid the effects of armed conflict, situations of generalized violence, violations of human rights or natural or human-made disasters, and who have not crossed an internationally recognized state border."[7]

While those forced from their homes in Libya are clearly IDPs, whether Libyans sheltering in Tunisia and other North African countries are in fact refugees is a matter of some debate. Under the 1951 Convention Relating to the Status of Refugees, a refugee is any person who, "owing to well-founded fear of being persecuted for reasons of race, religion, nationality, membership of a particular social group or political opinion, is outside the country of his nationality and is unable or, owing to such fear, is unwilling to avail himself of the protection of that country."[8] The 1969 Organization of African Unity (OAU) Convention Governing the Specific Aspects of Refugee Problems in Africa broadens this definition to also include those who flee due to "external aggression, occupation, foreign domination or events seriously disturbing public order in either part or the whole of his country of origin or nationality."[9] However, both conventions have exclusion clauses indicating that those who have committed crimes against peace, war crimes, crimes against humanity, serious nonpolitical crimes, or acts contrary to the principles and purposes of the UN and the OAU (now the African Union) are not eligible for refugee status.[10] As it stands, the vast majority of Libyans who have sought shelter in other North African states have not registered as asylum seekers or sought out formal refugee status. While it is likely that many would qualify for refugee status, this would need to be assessed through a reliable and fair refugee status determination process, bearing in mind the particular legal obligations undertaken by the relevant host country.[11] Accordingly, this book generally uses the term "exiles" to refer to Libyans who, for a variety of reasons, have left their country and cannot return but who have not necessarily sought or obtained recognition as refugees. Whether or not Libyans sheltering in neighboring states are recognized as refugees, they have a clear right not to be returned to their country if they may face grievous harms such as torture.[12]

Displacement situations are resolved through the pursuit of so-called durable solutions for refugees and IDPs. As the Inter-Agency Standing Committee's *Framework on Durable Solutions for Internally Displaced Persons* stresses, IDPs have the right to a durable solution to their displacement. This is achieved when they "no longer have any specific assistance and protection needs that are linked to their displacement and can enjoy their human rights without discrimination on account of their displacement."[13] Durable solutions for IDPs include voluntary return and reintegration, local integration into the communities where IDPs sought shelter, or settlement elsewhere in the state. A somewhat parallel set of solutions pertains for refugees who may voluntarily repatriate to their country of origin, locally integrate into their country of asylum, or resettle to another country. As citizens with the right to freedom of movement within their own countries, IDPs can in principle freely choose among the three durable solutions to displacement, although this is often difficult to realize in practice. In contrast, refugees have the right to return to their countries of origin but do not generally have an explicit legal right to local integration or third-country resettlement.

While legal and operational definitions structure responses to refugee and IDP flows, the terminology surrounding transitional justice and reconciliation processes is much murkier. Generally speaking, transitional justice may be understood as

> a set of measures that can be implemented to redress the legacies of massive human rights abuses that occur during armed conflict and under authoritarian regimes, where "redressing the legacies" means, primarily, giving force to human rights norms that were systematically violated. The different measures that together make up a holistic approach to transitional justice seek to provide recognition to victims, foster civic trust and promote possibilities for peace, reconciliation and democracy. They include criminal prosecutions of those most responsible for violations; reparations programs that distribute a

mix of material and symbolic benefits to victims (including compensation and apologies); restitution programs that seek to return housing, land and property to those who were dispossessed; truth-telling initiatives that investigate and report on periods of past abuse; and justice-sensitive security system reform that seeks to transform the military, police and judiciary responsibility for past violations.[14]

Particularly relevant to Libya, justice-sensitive security sector reform includes lustration or personnel-reform processes, which seek to remove those complicit in past abuses from official positions of power. Increasingly, transitional justice mechanisms are employed not only in the aftermath of conflict and abusive regimes, but also in the heat of ongoing violence.[15] However, this approach is contested, and in light of the civil war and fracturing of the Libyan government, the majority of the transitional justice processes initiated in the wake of the 2011 revolution have stalled.

Much as its proponents might hope, reconciliation does not necessarily flow naturally from transitional justice processes. Yet, in Libya as in many other conflict and postconflict contexts, many survivors insist that reconciliation is impossible in the absence of comprehensive truth-telling about atrocities and accountability for violations, which transitional justice processes seek to advance in different ways.[16] As a Libyan civil society activist expressed it, "How can we reconcile after all we suffered during and before the war? We can't. We have to talk about justice before we address reconciliation."[17] The civil war has fueled additional injustices, which further impede reconciliation prospects. Reconciliation eludes precise definition, as its meaning for different individuals and communities is shaped by varying experiences, histories, and cultural and moral commitments. However, reconciliation may be broadly understood as a *process* involving the (re)construction of "relationships of trust and cohesion."[18] This process may unfold on various levels, from the interpersonal and community levels to the national and international planes.[19]

Notes

1. Internal Displacement Monitoring Centre (IDMC), *Global Overview 2014: People Internally Displaced by Conflict and Violence* (Geneva: Norwegian Refugee Council, 2014), 61; IDMC, *Libya: Many IDPs Return but Concerns Persist for Certain Displaced Groups* (Geneva: Norwegian Refugee Council, 2011), 4–5; Office of the United Nations High Commissioner for Refugees (UNHCR), *Global Appeal 2012–2013* (Geneva: UNHCR, 2011).

2. Tarek Mitri, "Security Council Briefing," United Nations Support Mission in Libya (UNSMIL), August 27, 2014, http://unsmil.unmissions.org/Default.aspx?tabid=3543&ctl=Details&mid=6187&ItemID=1969772&language=en-US. See also "Humanitarian Aid for Displaced Families West of Tripoli," UNHCR, August 18, 2014, http://unsmil.unmissions.org/Default.aspx?ctl=Details&tabid=3543&mid=6187&ItemID=1964251.

3. IDMC, "Libya: State Collapse Triggers Mass Displacement," accessed May 15, 2015, http://www.internal-displacement.org/middle-east-and-north-africa/libya/2015/libya-state-collapse-triggers-mass-displacement.

4. Mitri, "Security Council Briefing."

5. Given our focus on the forced migration of Libyan citizens, we do not address the issue of increased trafficking from Libyan shores in detail in this work. It is important to recognize, however, that the rise of smuggling operations in post-Gaddafi Libya led to the deaths of more than twelve hundred people in the space of one week in April 2015, with one out of every sixteen migrants who attempted the trip in the first four months of 2015 perishing. Revived European Union funding for search-and-rescue operations in the Mediterranean since April 2015 has reduced the number of deaths, with an estimated two hundred thousand migrants and asylum seekers reaching Europe via the Mediterranean (including departures from Libya) in the summer of 2015; approximately twenty-one hundred died en route. See David Kirkpatrick, "200 Migrants Are Believed Drowned in Capsizing off Libya," *New York Times*, August 6, 2015, http://www.nytimes.com/2015/08/07/world/middleeast/200-migrants-are-believed-drowned-in-capsizing-off-libya.html?ref=topics; Alice Philipson, "'Dramatic' Fall in Mediterranean Migrant Deaths," *Telegraph*, June 10, 2015, http://www.telegraph.co.uk/news/worldnews/europe/italy/11731202/Revealed-Dramatic-fall-in-Mediterranean-migrant-deaths.html; Brookings Institution, "An Overlooked Crisis: Humanitarian Consequences of the Conflict in Libya," public event at Brookings Institution, Washington, DC, April 24, 2015, http://www.brookings.edu/events/2015/04/24-libya-displacement-overlooked-crisis; and Human Rights Watch, *The Mediterranean Migration Crisis: Why People Flee, What the EU Should Do* (New York: Human Rights Watch, 2015).

6. See Paul Salem and Amanda Kadlec, *Libya's Troubled Transition* (Beirut: Carnegie Middle East Center, 2012), and Ibrahim Sharqieh, *Reconstructing Libya: Stability through National Reconciliation* (Doha: Brookings Doha Center, 2013).

7. United Nations Economic and Social Council, "Human Rights, Mass Exoduses and Displaced Persons: Guiding Principles on Internal Displacement," Commission on Human Rights, Session 54, February 11, 1998, http://daccess-dds-ny.un.org/doc/UNDOC/GEN/G98/104/93/PDF/G9810493.pdf?OpenElement (E/CN.4/1998/53/Add.2), 5.

8. United Nations, "Convention Relating to the Status of Refugees," Treaty Series, July 28, 1951, http://www.ohchr.org/EN/ProfessionalInterest/Pages/StatusOfRefugees.aspx, Chapter 1, Article 1.A.(2).

9. Organization of African Unity (OAU), "Convention Governing the Specific Aspects of Refugee Problems in Africa," September 10, 1969, http://www.achpr.org/files/instruments/refugee-convention/achpr_instr_conv_refug_eng.pdf, Article 1.2.

10. See Article 1.F of the 1951 Refugee Convention and Article 1.5 of the 1969 OAU Convention.

11. Tunisia and Egypt are both parties to the 1951 Refugee Convention and the 1969 OAU Convention.

12. This right is, for example, articulated in Article 3 of the Convention against Torture. See United Nations General Assembly, "Convention against Torture and Other Cruel, Inhuman or Degrading Treatment or Punishment," Treaty Series, December 10, 1984, http://www.ohchr.org/EN/ProfessionalInterest/Pages/CAT.aspx. The main states hosting Libyan diaspora communities, including Tunisia and Egypt, are all parties to the Convention against Torture. More broadly, non-refoulement (not returning individuals to countries where they may face grave harm) is held by many to be a customary norm of international law.

13. Inter-Agency Standing Committee, *IASC Framework on Durable Solutions for Internally Displaced Persons* (Washington, DC: Brookings Institution–University of Bern Project on Internal Displacement, 2010), A-1.

14. Roger Duthie, "Transitional Justice and Displacement," *International Journal of Transitional Justice* 5, no. 2 (2011): 243; Pablo de Greiff, "Theorizing Transitional Justice," in *Transitional Justice: NOMOS LI*, ed. Melissa Williams, Rosemary Nagy, and Jon Elster (New York: New York University Press, 2012).

15. On the use of accountability and "transitional" justice mechanisms in the context of ongoing conflict, see, for example, Roberto Vidal López, "Truth-Telling, Internal Displacement, and the Peace Process in Colombia," in *Forced Migration, Reconciliation and Justice*, ed. Megan Bradley (Montreal: McGill–Queen's University Press, 2015).

16. Interviews undertaken in Yemen, Tunisia, and Libya for a comparative study of reconciliation in Middle Eastern countries following the region's recent uprisings suggest that the demand for truth-telling as a prerequisite for reconciliation is particularly strong in Libya. See Sharqieh, *Reconstructing Libya*, and Ibrahim Sharqieh, *A Lasting Peace? Yemen's Long Journey to National Reconciliation* (Doha: Brookings Doha Center, 2013).

17. Sharqieh, *Reconstructing Libya*, 6.

18. Joanna R. Quinn, "Introduction," in *Reconciliation(s): Transitional Justice in Postconflict Societies*, ed. Joanna R. Quinn (Montreal: McGill–Queen's University Press, 2009), 5.

19. Ibid. See also Megan Bradley, *Forced Migration, Reconciliation and Justice* (Montreal: McGill–Queen's University Press, 2015).

Chronology

February 17, 2011: Protests break out throughout Libya, and with particular intensity in Benghazi and Tripoli, against the Gaddafi regime. Regime forces violently repress peaceful protesters.

February 27, 2011: Anti-Gaddafi forces form the National Transitional Council in the liberated eastern city of Benghazi. It acted as an interim authority in the rebel-held areas of Libya. Meanwhile, violence forces hundreds of thousands of Libyans and foreign workers in Libya to escape the conflict into neighboring Tunisia and Egypt.

March 17, 2011: The UN Security Council passes Resolution 1973, imposing a no-fly zone over Libya, an arms embargo, and the freezing of assets owned by Libyan authorities among others. Resolution 1973 also establishes the legal basis for NATO's military intervention in Libya by demanding an immediate cease-fire, calling for the establishment of a no-fly zone, and authorizing international action to protect civilians. A previous resolution (1970), passed in February 2011, established a panel of experts to monitor sanctions implementation against Gaddafi regime officials and referred the situation in Libya to the prosecutor of the International Criminal Court.

March 19, 2011: NATO begins its military intervention in Libya.

April 2011: Libyans from the Nafusa Mountains flee into neighboring Tunisia following Gaddafi forces' attacks on their towns and villages.

June 27, 2011: The International Criminal Court issues arrest warrants against Gaddafi and several other senior regime officials.

August 2011: Tripoli falls to Libyan rebels. Gaddafi is forced to flee to his hometown of Sirte. Residents of Tawergha are displaced en masse.

October 20, 2011: Sirte and other remaining cities and areas controlled by pro-Gaddafi forces fall to rebel forces. The death of Gaddafi on October 20, 2011, marks the end of the Libyan Revolution.

February 2012: Misrata forces carry out deadly attacks against the Janzour Camp near Tripoli, which houses Tawerghan IDPs. Libyans mark the first anniversary of the Libyan Revolution.

July 2012: The first democratic elections in Libya are conducted. Members of the General National Congress (replacing the National Transitional Council) are tasked with the formation of a constituent assembly to write a new national constitution.

September 11, 2012: Heavily armed Islamist militiamen attack the US consulate in Benghazi and a CIA annex, killing four US citizens, including Ambassador J. Christopher Stevens.

October 10, 2013: Libyan prime minister Ali Zeidan is kidnapped by militia forces, then released several hours later.

November 23, 2013: Armed clashes intensify, particularly in Libyan cities, prompting declaration of a state of alert.

January 2014: Deadly clashes occur between Gaddafi loyalists and Libyan soldiers.

May 2014: Gen. Khalifa Hiftar launches Operation Dignity in eastern Libya with the stated aim of fighting terrorism, particularly targeting Islamist-leaning Libyan factions. The Libya Dawn coalition is formed to oppose Hiftar.

June 2014: Islamist parties lose in legislative elections in Libya to liberal factions. The newly elected House of Representatives is forced to relocate to Tobruk in the east after the Libya Dawn coalition refuses to recognize the outcome of the elections, later forming a Tripoli-based government.

July–August 2014: The Battle of the Tripoli International Airport is fought between the Libya Dawn coalition and the Zentan Brigades. Most of the airport and twenty planes are destroyed during the fighting. Hundreds of thousands of Libyans are displaced within and outside Libya due to ongoing, escalating violence.

January 2015: The UN-sponsored Geneva–Ghadamis talks brings members of the Tripoli-based General National Congress to meet with the Tobruk House of Representatives.

February 2015: Islamic State militants behead twenty-one Egyptian Coptic workers in Sirte, taken by the extremist group along with Derna in mid-2014. Egypt carries out air strikes on Islamic State positions in Libya.

June–August 2015: UN-backed peace talks take place in Skhirat, Morocco, between warring factions, leading to a deal to form a unity government. However, the Tripoli government boycotts the talks, which end in Geneva with no resolution.

August 2015: Islamic State forces brutally quell a rebellion in Sirte. The Tobruk government calls for the Arab League to conduct air strikes against Islamic State positions in Sirte. The Arab League pledges military support for Libya.

Libya's Displacement Crisis

*Uprooted by Revolution
and Civil War*

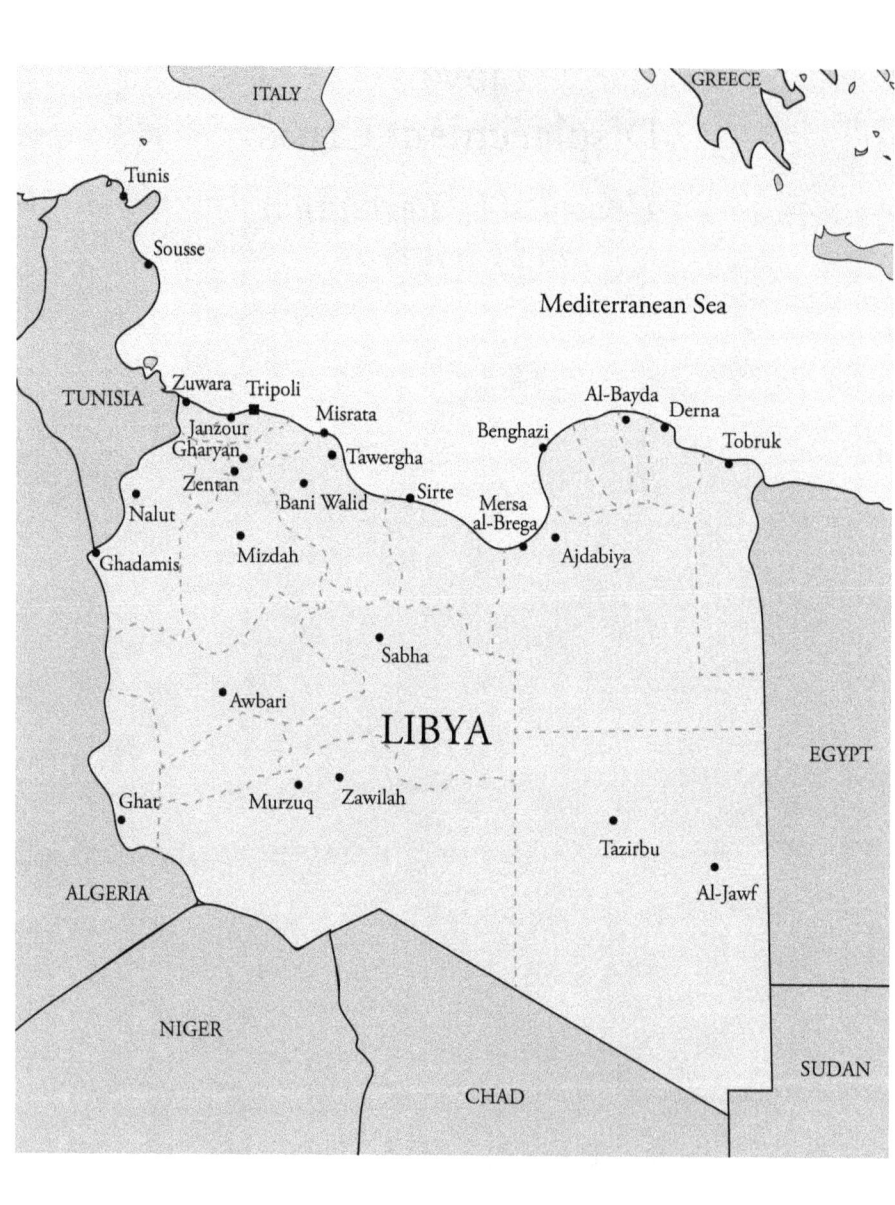

1

Background

A Fallen Regime, Victor's Justice, and Resurgent Violence

SPANNING MORE THAN FOUR DECADES, Gaddafi's rule was characterized by overlapping layers of human rights abuses. The regime's "signature violations" included the criminalization of dissent, mock trials, extrajudicial executions, torture, disappearances, and the fostering of tribal and ethnic divisions, which continue to fuel unrest and displacement today.[1] Rhetorically, the regime was committed to the redistribution of resources, including housing and land, to promote greater equality, but in practice land restitution and property policies were used to shore up Gaddafi's power. Ambiguous and arbitrary policies and legal frameworks rendered property relations and tenure security precarious, further feeding the discontent that drove Libyans to the streets in protest.[2]

The Fall of the Gaddafi Regime

Government forces opened fire on opposition protestors in Benghazi on February 17, 2011, sparking violent uprisings that were met with crushing regime retaliation. In the face of escalating violence and violations of international humanitarian and human rights law, the UN Security Council adopted Resolution 1973, establishing a no-fly zone over Libya and calling for "all the necessary measures to protect civilians." On March 24, 2011, a North Atlantic Treaty Organization (NATO) mission was launched to police the no-fly zone and target government forces on the ground.[3] Gaddafi's death in late October 2011 and the flight of several of his family members and top officials completed the regime's fall from power. The commission of inquiry created by the UN Human Rights Council to investigate violations against civilians during the conflict concluded in its June 2011 report that the government and, on a more limited scale, the rebels committed war crimes and crimes against humanity over the course of the nine-month struggle. These crimes included the destruction of towns such as Tawergha following the complete expulsion of its population.[4]

The European Union in particular made significant investments in Libya's transition process for geopolitical reasons, but overall international engagement in post-Gaddafi Libya may best be characterized as a "light-footprint" approach.[5] There was initially some optimism surrounding the transition process, particularly following the July 2012 elections.[6] Ultimately, however, this light-footprint approach proved out of step with the scale of the challenges the country faced, from the establishment of stability, security, and a democratic government and the reform of the civil service, to the development of nuanced measures and strategies to deal with the widespread injustices of the Gaddafi regime and the fresh injustices committed during the conflict. In the absence of unifying leadership and sufficient, sustained international support, Libya has descended into pervasive insecurity. This is reflected in incidents that include the militant attack on the US mission in Benghazi in September 2012 in which Ambassador J. Christopher Stevens was killed, the kidnapping of the Libyan prime minister in October 2013, the erection of port blockades choking the national economy, and the escalation of violence in the summer of 2014, leading to the outbreak of civil war. We discuss the civil war in more detail below, but, in short, fighting in the summer of 2014 between militias affiliated with the Libya Dawn coalition and forces backing returned Libyan general Khalifa Hiftar (linked in part to disputes over the outcomes of the June 2014 elections, which saw losses for Islamist parties) prompted the withdrawal of the vast majority of international actors from Libya, including staff of the UN Support Mission in Libya (UNSMIL) and humanitarian agencies.[7] Unchecked violence, the massive proliferation of small arms, and the fracturing of the government have only amplified Libyans' longstanding lament that "*ma fish qanoun*" (there is no law).[8]

The Rise of Victor's Justice

Even before the outbreak of civil war, establishing rule of law in Libya represented an enormous struggle, rooted significantly in the deep deficiencies of the Gaddafi-era system, which nurtured popular expectations that "justice" be swift, politicized, and retributive. Against this backdrop, long delays in bringing perpetrators to account for their actions have heightened grievances, and undercut the state as militias—many of which are on the state's payroll—have enforced their own brand of extrajudicial justice, apprehending alleged "anti-revolutionary figures," running prisons, and undertaking interrogations, often involving torture followed by executions.[9] Thousands of individuals captured during and after the revolution remain in detention, often without charge, in makeshift, militia-run prisons.[10] While some detainees were likely complicit in abuses of the Gaddafi regime, many are simply on the losing ends of local rivalries or vendettas.

Since the end of the revolution, efforts to assert control over the militias have been complicated by disagreements over their proper role in post-Gaddafi Libya. Former prime minister Ali Zeidan, for example, viewed them as a cause of violence and advocated for them to be disbanded, for their members to be integrated into formal systems, and for any detainees under their control to be transferred to government facilities. In contrast, others see the militias as playing an important part in preserving the revolution, particularly until pro-Gaddafi officials are completely purged from the government.[11] In any case, as the outbreak of civil war has made all too clear, formal state institutions lack the capacity to wrest power from influential militias, whose approach to settling scores in post-Gaddafi Libya drives further displacement. The militias' role in generating fresh displacement crises even before the start of the civil war is illustrated by the October 2012 militia assault on the town of Bani Walid, where residents refused to give up alleged perpetrators, leading to the displacement of ten thousand families and the death of at least fifty people.[12]

As UNSMIL has pointed out, improving Libya's security situation, addressing grievances, and advancing reconciliation are deeply intertwined challenges.[13] The Political Isolation Law (No. 13/2013) passed in 2013 mandates the exclusion from public office of broad swaths of the population, often with very limited connection to the previous regime. This law has since been repealed by the parliament in Tobruk, but in any case on a deeper level the fundamental "question of who should be held responsible for sustaining the totalitarian regime, beyond the senior leadership, remains unresolved. Addressing past crimes and crimes committed during the Revolution" and afterward "is complicated by the fact that large numbers of Libyans from different walks of life are potentially implicated."[14] During the revolution and afterward, some victims of the previous regime became perpetrators of abuse and vice versa, particularly as many actors have now turned to violence in the contest over competing visions for post-Gaddafi Libya. Some have suggested that the upsurge in violence since 2014 and the creation of new alliances in the civil war have done away with the "culture of division" of the country into *thuwar* (revolutionaries) and *azlam* (Gaddafi cronies) that dominated Libyan politics in the early years after the revolution.[15] For example, a former Gaddafi officer who returned from Tunisia in the summer of 2014 to fight alongside Zentani militiamen who were his enemies in 2011 opined that "it is not pro- or anti-Gaddafi any more—it is about Libya."[16] However, upon closer examination, the continued relevance of this deep-rooted culture of division is clear, even if its implications have morphed as new incentives have emerged for rivals to overlook their mutual grievances—however temporarily. Not only individuals but whole communities continue to be labeled *thuwar* (for example, Misrata, Zentan, Benghazi, Zawiyah, Zuwara, and Souq al-Jumma) or *azlam* (for example, sections of Bani Walid, Western Rayayneh, Werfella, and Mashashya). This perpetuates the attribution of collective responsibility for individual wrongdoing and risks recreating a system that, like Gaddafi's regime, privileges particular groups while marginalizing others.[17]

This culture of division is evident in the legal framework related to transitional justice issues that was developed in the early aftermath of the revolution. Set out in several related laws, this framework was developed by the victors of the revolution and fails—or at best struggles—to attend to the claims of those perceived as *azlam*, including the majority of those whose displacement is becoming protracted. In May 2012, with the adoption of Law 38/2012 on Special Procedures during the Transitional Period, the National Transitional Council (NTC) granted amnesty to "revolutionaries" for "military, security and civil acts required by the 17 February Revolution" and that were undertaken with the "purpose of leading the revolution to victory."[18] In contrast, the sweeping Political Isolation Law excluded from public office for ten years those who served the former regime, even in relatively low-ranking positions, significantly draining the pool of job candidates with bureaucratic experience and "swelling the number of 'losers' of the transition."[19]

Law 17/2012 on National Reconciliation and Transitional Justice established the Fact-Finding and Reconciliation Committee, also known as the Truth-Seeking and Reconciliation Body. Mandated to investigate cases of past abuses from 1969 onward, the commission can recommend reparations including financial compensation and refer cases for criminal prosecution. However, the commission has undertaken only limited activities to date, and its staff report that in practice they do not have the capacity to investigate post-2011 violations given the sensitivity of these cases and the insecure environment, particularly since the beginning of the civil war. Law 17/2012 was criticized for its limited scope, its failure to clearly articulate the goals of the transitional justice process, and its inadequate focus on the rights and needs of victims. It was therefore replaced by the Law on Transitional Justice passed by the General National Congress (GNC) on September 22, 2013.

This newer law further elaborates on the mandate of the Fact-Finding and Reconciliation Committee and clarifies that the transitional justice process "is meant to address the serious and systematic abuses of fundamental rights, committed by state agencies and suffered by Libyans under the former regime. This would take place through social, administrative and judicial procedures that aim at revealing the truth, holding offenders accountable, preserving national memories and redressing any wrongdoing for which the state is responsible."[20] The objective of the process is to "preserve and strengthen civil peace, deter human rights violations, reassure and convince people that justice exists, and that it is effective, identify the responsibility of state bodies or any other parties for human rights violations, document and preserve events covered by transitional justice then deliver them to the competent national authorities, compensate victims and affected persons, achieve community reconciliations and reform institutions."[21] The law covers the period from September 1, 1969, when Gaddafi seized power, to the "end of [the] Transitional period following elections to the legislative council" and includes "some effects of the February 17 Revolution," such as "acts that were necessary to protect the Revolution but showed conduct inconsistent with its principles, reconciliation, establishing social peace and laying the foundation for a state of rights and law."[22] The law therefore opens up some space for consideration of the violations inflicted during and after the revolution that fueled some of Libya's still unresolved displacement. Given the outbreak of the civil war, however, efforts to implement this law, and related transitional justice and accountability processes, have largely stalled. Even if the transitional justice process were to be revived, the law's predominant focus on abuses perpetrated by state agencies under the former regime suggests that it will be difficult to use the law to ensure that violations perpetrated by anti-Gaddafi forces and by the wide range of parties involved in civil war—including those that compelled the displaced to flee their homes—are taken seriously.[23]

Further, the law does not address property restitution, an aspect of transitional justice that is of particular relevance to displaced populations.

The marginalization of displaced Libyans and their concerns in the country's transitional justice framework is not exceptional. Historically, transitional justice processes have not often engaged with IDPs, refugees, and other diaspora community members as key stakeholders, nor have they tended to consider displacement as a harm meriting attention and redress in its own right. This trend is gradually changing, in part due to the growing recognition that effectively tailored transitional justice and reconciliation processes can make significant, if inevitably limited, contributions to supporting the resolution of displacement.[24] Within this context, as the following sections demonstrate, Libya stands out as a country in which the connections between transitional justice, reconciliation, the restoration of security, and the resolution of displacement are particularly stark. Although the country's fledgling transitional justice process has to a significant extent been arrested by the incapacitation of various governmental bodies with the outbreak of increased levels of violence in 2014, when greater stability eventually returns to Libya, concerns surrounding transitional justice and accountability for past wrongs will unavoidably move back up the political agenda. As it stands, the existing legal framework for transitional justice in Libya is, as discussed above, highly flawed. This period therefore provides an important opportunity to consider how this system (and the role of the international community in supporting transitional justice in Libya) may be revamped, with a view to ensuring that the process is equitable and responds in a meaningful way to the concerns of diverse groups in Libyan society, including those whose displacement has become long-standing.

The Initial Displacement Crisis

During the nine-month revolution, the collapse of public order, sieges on urban areas, and street-to-street fighting resulted in the flight of over 1.3 million Libyan citizens, migrant workers, asylum seekers, and refugees long resident in Libya.[25] Neighboring Tunisia and Egypt were particularly popular destinations, with an estimated 255,000 Libyans seeking shelter in Tunisia by June 2011, in addition to some 152,000 who entered Egypt. As of 2012, the Office of the United Nations High Commissioner for Refugees (UNHCR) reported that more than 660,000 Libyans had fled the country, although only 3,322 Libyans worldwide were formally recognized as refugees as of January 2014.[26]

Instead of seeking formal refugee status, the majority of Libyans who fled the country simply entered neighboring states such as Tunisia that do not require Libyans to have a visa for visits of less than three months. In line with the region's tradition of providing shelter to displaced "brothers" without necessarily according formal refugee status, fleeing Libyans met with relatively little initial resistance, particularly as many had some financial resources at their disposal and were thus able to find accommodations in hotels or rental properties.[27] In addition, many sought shelter with host families; a smaller proportion was housed in temporary camps established in southern Tunisia. Return was the predominant "solution" for the initial wave of those who sought shelter outside the country, although little information is available on these return movements as they were generally undertaken by families independent of extensive external support.

In addition to those who fled the country, hundreds of thousands were displaced within Libya. UNHCR estimated that by October 2011 there were some 150,000 IDPs in Libya, down from approximately 550,000 at the peak of the crisis.[28] Many families were subjected to multiple displacements. Most commonly, IDPs took shelter with relatives, friends, or other host families or in public buildings, hotels, resorts, construction sites, or factories.[29] As citizens of a middle-income country, many Libyans IDPs, like those who fled the country, had at least modest financial resources at their disposal. This strengthened the capacity of many families to weather the initial crisis of their displacement and to return to and repair their homes in relatively short order, often as soon as fighting moved on from their areas of origin. Supplementing the personal resources families used to meet their needs, both the former government and the NTC endeavored to assist the majority of the displaced in the areas under their control. Beyond opening their homes to the displaced, as encouraged by local customs of hospitality, many Libyans participated as volunteers in efforts to respond to the crisis, including by repairing buildings, assisting at hospitals and clinics, and providing child care.[30] International actors, including UN agencies, the International Organization for Migration (IOM), Arab states, regional organizations, and a range of NGOs, were also involved in providing emergency aid. Meeting humanitarian needs promptly and avoiding the sustained, catastrophic impoverishment of the majority of the displaced increased the ability of many of Libya's IDPs to return to their homes without extended delays.

Despite the fairly prompt resolution of the majority of the initial Libyan displacement situation, two key forced migration scenarios persist—one internal and one external. These displacement situations are rapidly evolving in light of heightened violence that has accompanied the descent into civil war.

Civil War and the Reescalation of the Displacement Crisis

The sudden collapse of the Gaddafi regime generated numerous challenges, including, but not limited to, constitution drafting, transitional justice, institutional reform, and the reintegration of ex-combatants—the revolutionaries who fought against the Gaddafi regime. The latter challenge was particularly pronounced, and the failure to meet it has had dire consequences for Libya's security. Since the 2011 revolution, approximately two hundred thousand revolutionaries have become affiliated with various militias, many of which have now taken control of different parts of the country. The prevalence of militias in Libya has undermined the government's authority, weakened security to unprecedented levels, and exacerbated the displacement crisis to an alarming extent.

During the Libyan uprising, the various revolutionaries united against a common enemy, the Gaddafi regime. However, once that common enemy was defeated, Libya's militias turned against each other. Instead of filling the security gaps created by the regime's collapse, competition among revolutionaries actually widened them. Driven by their own agendas, revolutionaries started to combat each other and compete for power and resources. As Libya is a resource-rich country, militia commanders had strong material incentives to maintain their own forces (enabling them to control resource flows), rather than disarming them and joining state institutions.

In May 2014, retired general Khalifa Hiftar, who also fought against Gaddafi in 2011, launched what came to be known as Operation Dignity, a campaign that aimed to "cleanse" Libya of "terrorism." Based in the eastern part of the country, Operation Dignity started to attack both 17 February revolutionaries (those who fought against Gaddafi) and Ansar al-Sharia, a Salafi Jihadist militia based in Benghazi. These two groups united with several others to resist Hiftar's campaign, forming an alliance called the Shura Council of Benghazi Revolutionaries. In western Libya, General Hiftar formed an alliance with the powerful militia of the town of Zentan to fight Islamists. The Zentan militia are motivated more by tribal than ideological commitments and fought aggressively against the Gaddafi regime. An alliance to counter Hiftar also emerged in the west, named Fajr Libya, or Libya Dawn. It includes the powerful Misrata militia, groups such as the Libya Revolutionary Operations Room and Libya Shield Force, militias of other tribes such as Zawiyah and Sabrata, the city of Zuwara, and some towns in the Nafusa Mountains in western Libya, including Nalut and Gharyan. Though involving mostly tribal and regional forces, this alliance came to be known as an Islamist force because it includes some Islamist groups. Libya Dawn is determined to fight General Hiftar and his allies in the west of Libya, especially Zentan's two most powerful brigades, Qaaqaa and Sawaeq. The outcome of all of these developments is that Libya is enduring a brutal civil war fought predominantly between Hiftar's Operation Dignity and Fajr Libya. Figure 1 maps the major players in Libya's civil war.

In the context of the ongoing, violent contestation of power, Libya's most prominent state institution, its parliament, which had been known as the GNC, has been divided between the two camps. Following the June 2014 parliamentary elections, Libya ended up with two parliaments: the GNC in Tripoli that existed before the elections and is supported by Fajr Libya, and the postelection House of Representatives (HoR) that allied with General Hiftar and relocated to the eastern city of Tobruk. Within the HoR, there have been signs of division and splitting in protest of Hiftar's handling of Operation Dignity. Hiftar's management became contentious: While some members clearly opposed him, others had their reservations, and a third faction supported him. In any case, both parliaments operated simultaneously and independently of each other, and of course each accused the other of being illegitimate. Similarly, each parliament elected a prime minister, with Omar al-Hassi heading the government in Tripoli and Abdullah al-Thani leading the one in Tobruk. Obviously, such a state of polarization is not conducive to the development of a comprehensive security strategy or transitional justice program, or making other serious efforts that could mitigate or resolve the displacement problem.

The brutal civil war in Libya has had a serious impact on the humanitarian crisis in Libya and on the country's refugees and IDPs in particular. By some estimates, over 2,800 people were killed in the violence in 2014; in January through May 2015, over 750 people were reportedly killed.[31] In addition to forcing hundreds of thousands more people to flee their homes, the war has pushed the protracted displacement of Libyans uprooted in 2011 much farther down the list of priorities in Libya. In many ways, the primary challenge of the post-Gaddafi era has shifted from reconstruction and resolution of national challenges that were created in the process of regime change—such as the displacement problem—to attempting to manage a civil war that has splintered the government and devastated large parts of the country, including neighborhoods in the two biggest cities of Tripoli and Benghazi. Trying to "put out the fire" and prevent the war from escalating has become the issue that receives the most attention from the various Libyan stakeholders, including the fractured government, civil society, political parties, and tribes, as well as the international community and other external stakeholders.

Those displaced by the uprising against Gaddafi are perceived as less relevant to this civil war, and public debate has started to include instead those displaced by the new civil war. The newly displaced entering the public debate and receiving the militias' attention is to be expected, as focusing on this human tragedy has become a way to promote the parties' agendas. For example, there were debates in Libya about the Libyans uprooted by the new civil war, especially in the Wersheffana area in the summer of 2014 after a brutal battle that targeted the tribe and resulted in the displacement of much of its population, both internally and outside Libya. In addition, debates also arose regarding the Libyans displaced by the fighting between Hiftar's forces and the Shura Council in Benghazi. Even the international community became primarily focused on the fighting and concerns about possible spillover to neighboring countries, rather than on the well-being of the displaced themselves. In September 2014, for example, Tunisia and Algeria launched a joint effort to prevent Libya's conflict from expanding into their territory.[32] Tunisia, in particular, focused its efforts on preventing groups and individuals infiltrating its land to carry out what it called "terrorist operations."[33]

The current vicious civil war in Libya has, to a large extent, been balanced between the major combatants, and thus a military solution or decisive victory is unlikely. Many of the parties to the civil war enjoy strong external support from regional players, none of whom is willing to easily concede defeat. In such circumstances, a dialogue or a negotiated settlement is the most feasible option that is in the interest of all parties. The UN-sponsored peace talks led by Bernardino Leon are a clear representation of a national dialogue that could provide a formula to end Libya's civil war. In these talks and any future national dialogue, the displaced communities—both IDPs and exiles—must be sufficiently represented, and any future agreements must take their plight into account.

A particularly significant concern that has been exacerbated by the civil war is the lack of accessible and effective venues through which to pursue accountability for abuses—including systematic displacement—of the

Gaddafi era, the 2011 revolution, and the subsequent violence. Local, national, regional, and international mechanisms all have contributions to make (depending on the nature of the violations) in tackling the culture of impunity that has characterized Libya during and after the Gaddafi regime. However, all of these mechanisms have their limitations, many of which have become particularly pronounced since the upsurge in violence and the fracturing of governance structures in Libya. For example, Human Rights Watch has stressed that the Libyan judiciary is near collapse, with many courts suspending their work owing to the erosion of security and targeted attacks on prosecutors and judges.[34] UNHCR has indicated that it is "deeply disturbed" by death sentences handed down by a Tripoli-based court in July 2015 against several former senior members of the Gaddafi regime, especially as many defendants were subjected to torture and lacked access to legal counsel.[35] Customary or traditional justice mechanisms, including those mediated by tribal leaders, have a long-standing role in addressing justice concerns in Libya and may make important contributions to addressing violations, including those associated with displacement.[36] However, the authority of tribal leaders and their ability to enforce agreements reached through customary processes has been challenged and in some cases undermined by new militia groups, undercutting the extent to which these avenues can be used as alternatives to more formal legal channels. In light of the considerable limitations facing local and national justice mechanisms, some advocates have called for the International Criminal Court (ICC) to take a more active role in investigating and prosecuting serious abuses in Libya.[37] At present, the ICC has only one open case in Libya, the prosecution of Gaddafi's son, Saif al-Islam Gaddafi, on charges of murder and persecution. As Human Rights Watch points out, many of the human rights violations currently taking place in Libya, including forced displacement, may be "sufficiently widespread to amount to crimes against humanity."[38] However, owing to pervasive insecurity, lack of resources, and obstruction on the part of Libyan authorities and militias (including those holding Saif al-Islam Gaddafi), the ICC has struggled to effectively advance its current case against him, never mind investigate ongoing crimes in Libya as authorized by a unanimous UN Security Council resolution.[39] Despite the present barriers to using local, national, regional, and international venues to uphold accountability for violations, it is important to stress that actors on all sides have been complicit in violations and that under international law not only state officials and agencies, but also nonstate actors can and should be held responsible for grave breeches of human rights and humanitarian law, including those associated with displacement.[40]

In short, while the initial displacement crisis that accompanied the revolution was, for the most part, resolved quite rapidly, the civil war has fueled new displacements and undermined durable solutions and the pursuit of accountability for those who were uprooted during the revolution. As elaborated in the following sections, the persistent internal and cross-border displacement situations are intimately tied to postrevolution security failures and problematic approaches to transitional justice and reconciliation. Divisions between perceived loyalists, opponents of the fallen regime, and new power brokers are a central element of many of Libya's ongoing displacement cases. However, a range of other elements also shape exposure to forced migration and access to durable solutions, including race and tribal relations, land disputes, and other historical grievances.[41] Responding effectively to these ongoing internal and cross-border displacement situations has been complicated by the fact that while forced migration has taken place in different ways throughout modern Libyan history, the scale and complexity of the issue has grown, outpacing the capacity and clout of the fractured post-Gaddafi state.

Notes

1. UNSMIL, "Transitional Justice: Foundation for a New Libya," United Nations, September 17, 2012, https://unsmil.unmissions.org/LinkClick.aspx?fileticket=8XrRUO-sXBs%3D&tabid=3543&language=en-US; International Crisis Group (ICG), *Divided We Stand: Libya's Enduring Conflicts* (New York: ICG, 2012), 1.

2. For a thorough discussion of Gaddafi's manipulation of housing and land policies and restitution processes, see Rhodri C. Williams, *Housing, Land and Property Issues and the Response to Displacement in Libya* (Geneva: UNHCR, 2012).

3. For discussion of the NATO mission and the international community's subsequent "light-footprint" approach in Libya, see Christopher S. Chivvis, *Toppling Qaddafi: Libya and the Limits of Liberal Intervention* (Cambridge: Cambridge University Press, 2013).

4. United Nations Human Rights Council, *Report of the International Commission of Inquiry on Libya* (Geneva: United Nations Human Rights Council, 2012).

5. Chivvis, *Toppling Qaddafi*.

6. For examples of such perspectives, see, for instance, Dirk Vandervalle, "After Qaddafi: The Surprising Success of the New Libya," *Foreign Affairs* 91, no. 6 (2012), and Jason Pack, "Democracy Is Messy—Especially in Libya," *Guardian*, October 9, 2012.

7. Following the June 2014 vote, the newly elected House of Representatives convened in Tobruk, as forces backing the Islamist parties who lost ground in the election were in control of Tripoli. Many Islamist legislators boycotted the session. On the urging of Fajr Libya coalition members, the former General National Congress reconvened in Tripoli in August 2014, despite its expired mandate, and named Omar al-Hassi as prime minister. See Mitri, "Security Council Briefing." On the return of Hiftar, see, for example, Ibrahim Sharqieh, "Beware Libya's 'Fair Dictator,'" *New York Times*, June 23, 2014, http://www.nytimes.com/2014/06/24/opinion/beware-libyas-fair-dictator.html?_r=0. For a discussion of the complex relationship between the militias and the Libyan state, see Frederic Wehrey, "What's Behind Libya's Spiraling Violence?," *Washington Post*, July 28, 2014, http://www.washingtonpost.com/blogs/monkey-cage/wp/2014/07/28/whats-behind-libyas-spiraling-violence/.

8. ICG, *Trial by Error: Justice in Post-Qadhafi Libya* (New York: ICG, 2013), 6.

9. Ibid., i, 4, 35; Amnesty International, *Militias Threaten Hope for New Libya* (London: Amnesty International, 2012).

10. ICG, *Trial by Error*, 4; International Legal Assistance Consortium (ILAC), *ILAC Rule of Law Assessment Report: Libya 2013* (Stockholm: ILAC, 2013), 34.

11. ICG, *Trial by Error*, ii.

12. Ibid., 1.

13. UNSMIL is tasked with building the capacity of the Libyan government and supporting its efforts to transition to democracy, promote human rights and rule of law, increase arms control, and counter weapons proliferation. See UNSMIL, "UNSMIL Mandate," accessed September 28, 2014, http://unsmil.unmissions.org/. With the upsurge in violence in Libya in 2014, UNSMIL staff were evacuated from the country in July 2014, along with the staff of the vast majority of other international organizations and international NGOs. See "Libya Insecurity Forces Aid Workers to Leave," IRIN, August 7, 2014, http://www.irinnews.org/report/100455/libya-insecurity-forces-aid-workers-to-leave.

14. UNSMIL, "Transitional Justice." See also "Libya Revokes Bill Which Banned Gaddafi-Era Officials from Office," BBC, http://www.bbc.com/news/world-latin-america-31104099.

15. These divisions are further complicated by competing visions of issues such as the role of Islam in Libyan politics, as reflected in General Hiftar's return to Libya and the violence that has accompanied his marshaling and deployment of armed forces opposed to actors associated with the Muslim Brotherhood.

16. David D. Kirkpatrick, "Strife in Libya Could Presage Long Civil War," *New York Times*, August 24, 2014, http://www.nytimes.com/2014/08/25/world/africa/libyan-unrest.html?_r=0.

17. Sharqieh, *Reconstructing Libya*, 1, 4.

18. ICG, *Trial by Error*, 28. The NTC was replaced by the elected General National Congress on August 8, 2012.

19. Roman David and Houda Mzioudet, *Personnel Change or Personal Change? Rethinking Libya's Political Isolation Law* (Doha: Brookings Doha Center / Stanford Center on Democracy, Development and the Rule of Law, 2014), 1.

20. "Draft Law on Transitional Justice," as quoted in Human Rights Watch, *Priorities for Legislative Reform: A Human Rights Roadmap for a New Libya* (New York: Human Rights Watch, 2014), 42.

21. Ibid., 43.

22. Ibid.

23. Some rebels and officials associated with the revolution argue that residents were not physically compelled to flee but rather "chose" to move due to their fears of retaliation and retribution. It is important to recognize that under international standards, including the UN Guiding Principles on Internal Displacement, individuals who leave their homes under such threatening circumstances are considered to have been displaced. That is, displacement can be caused not only by overt physical force, but also by fear of imminent violence. See Walter Kälin, *The Guiding Principles on Internal Displacement: Annotations*, 2nd ed. (Washington, DC: American Society of International Law, 2008).

24. On the connections between displacement and transitional justice, see, for example, Roger Duthie, ed., *Displacement and Transitional Justice* (New York: Social Science Research Council, 2012); Megan Bradley *Displacement, Reconciliation and Transitional Justice: Assumptions, Challenges and Lessons*, Forced Migration Policy Briefing 9 (Oxford: Refugee Studies Centre, 2012); Megan Bradley, *Refugee Repatriation: Justice, Responsibility and Redress* (Cambridge: Cambridge University Press, 2013); and Megan Bradley, *Forced Migration, Reconciliation and Justice*.

25. Before the crisis, an estimated 1.5 to 2.5 million foreign migrants were resident in Libya. By late August 2011, almost 670,000 of them had fled the country, but many could not return to their countries of origin for a range of reasons, including ongoing conflicts. See IDMC, *Libya: Many IDPs Return*, 4–5. While not a focus of this report, the large-scale displacement of migrants working in Libya presented a major political and humanitarian challenge. As these individuals did not generally qualify for refugee protection, their legal status and responsibility for assisting them was unclear. However, coordinated efforts between host governments, states of origin, and international organizations including the International Organization for Migration resulted in a response that is broadly seen as a success, prompting the development of new frameworks to inform similar future situations. For discussion of this aspect of the Libyan displacement situation, see Khalid Koser, "Protecting Non-citizens in Situations of Conflict, Violence and Disasters," in *Humanitarian Crises and Migration*, ed. Susan Forbes Martin, Sanjula S. Weerasinghe, and Abbie Taylor (New York: Routledge, 2014).

26. UNHCR, *Global Appeal* 2012–2013.

27. On historical responses to forced migration in the Middle East, see, for example, Dawn Chatty, *Displacement and Dispossession in the Modern Middle East* (Cambridge: Cambridge University Press, 2010).

28. IDMC, *Libya: Many IDPs Return*, 4; IDMC, *Global Overview 2014*, 61.

29. IDMC, *Libya: Many IDPs Return*, 5.

30. Ibid., 7.

31. Borzou Daragahi, "More than 100,000 Killed in One of Middle East's Bloodiest Years," *Financial Times*, January 2, 2015, http://www.ft.com/intl/cms/s/0/c2b6329a-9287-11e4-b213-00144feabdc0.html#axzz3n3UE5eQN. See also data collected by Libyan Body Count, an independent NGO, http://www.libyabodycount.org/table.

32. See "Tansiq Tunisi Jiza'iri litafadi tawassuʻ ruqʻat al-qital al-Libi" [Tunisian Algerian coordination to prevent expansion of Libyan fighting], *Libya Almostakbal*, September 20, 2014, http://libya-al-mostakbal.org/news/clicked/55703.

33. Ibid.

34. Human Rights Watch, "Libya: New ICC Investigation Needed amid Crisis," May 11, 2015, https://www.hrw.org/news/2015/05/11/libya-new-icc-investigation-needed-amid-crisis.

35. "Libya Trial: Gaddafi Son Sentenced to Death over War Crimes," BBC News, July 28, 2015, http://www.bbc.com/news/world-africa-33688391; D. Kirkpatrick, "Son of Muammar el-Qaddafi Sentenced to Death in Libya," *New York Times*, July 28, 2015, http://www.nytimes.com/2015/07/29/world/africa/seif-al-islam-el-qaddafi-death-sentence-libya.html?_r=0.

36. Ibrahim Sharqieh, "Vengeance Has No Place in a Libya Free of Qaddafi," *The National*, October 6, 2011, http://www.thenational.ae/thenationalconversation/comment/vengeance-has-no-place-in-a-libya-free-of-qaddafi.

37. Human Rights Watch, "Libya: New ICC Investigation Needed."

38. Ibid.

39. Prosecuting the crime of forced displacement under international law through the ICC poses particularly pronounced difficulties from the evidentiary perspective. On this issue, see, for example, Paige Morrow and Jennifer Winstanley, "The Challenge of Prosecuting Forced Displacement at the International Criminal Court," in *Forced Migration, Reconciliation and Justice*, ed. Megan Bradley (Montreal: McGill–Queen's University Press, 2015), 276–97.

40. Mondher Cherni, secretary-general, Organisation Contre la Torture en Tunisie, interview with the author, Tunis, Tunisia, July 7, 2015.

41. Sharqieh, *Reconstructing Libya*, 20; ICG, *Divided We Stand*, 4. In some instances, long-standing tribal disputes were pushed to the forefront by divisions between loyalists and anti-Gaddafi groups. This has included, for example, tribal disputes in the Western Mountains (Nafusa) and between the people of Misrata and those of Bani Walid.

2

A Growing Crisis

Internal Displacement in Post-Gaddafi Libya

FOUR YEARS AFTER the revolution, Libya has become a patchwork of displacement. By the end of 2013, an estimated 59,400 Libyans were uprooted within their own country; by the fall of 2014, conservative estimates put the number of IDPs in Libya at over 100,000.[1] While the ongoing civil war complicates the collection of reliable data on displacement, by March 2015, according to the Internal Displacement Monitoring Centre (IDMC), the number of IDPs in Libya had quadrupled to over 400,000.[2] UNHCR has estimated that some 56,000 of these IDPs are people who were still displaced as a result of the 2011 uprising.[3] In terms of the regional distribution of IDPs, IDMC indicates that at least 269,000 Libyans fled the violence in western Libya starting in mid-May 2014, that 90,000 were displaced in the east since mid-July 2014, and that another 18,500 people from southern Libya had been uprooted within the country as of January 15, 2015.[4] Most of these IDPs scattered across thirty-five towns and cities, sheltering in schools and other public places.[5]

The increased number of displaced people has of course had a serious impact on the previously existing displacement situation as the newcomers place additional stress on extremely limited humanitarian resources. To deal with Libya's new wave of displacement, the UN launched an appeal in September 2014 to raise $35.25 million to fund life-saving and humanitarian assistance, but according to the UN there has been virtually no response from donors.[6] The vast majority of international organizations and NGOs have now pulled out of Libya, leaving the humanitarian response to a small number of NGOs and the Libyan Red Crescent.[7]

Many of those IDPs who were uprooted in the context of the recent violence may be able to return to their homes relatively promptly upon the restoration of a reasonable degree of security, as occurred for many IDPs temporarily uprooted during the revolution. However, for those who have been internally displaced for a longer period, their uprooting has often had a distinctly retributive character, as expulsion has been used to punish families and communities labeled as loyalists. In other instances, displacement has been caused or sustained for material gain, exploiting the vulnerability of those who were disempowered by the Gaddafi regime's fall. For example, in the Nafusa Mountains, tribes including the Rayayneh and Mashashya have been displaced through postconflict reprisals motivated by retribution for perceived Gaddafi loyalism, in combination with grudges over land and water access.[8] Many Tuareg forced from their homes in the desert town of Ghadamis in the summer of 2011 remain displaced; some opponents of their return have argued that the Tuareg are not Libyans but Malians, in an attempt to undercut their claims.[9] Residents of the towns of Tiji and Badr in the Baten Al Jabal area were attacked by Amazighs from Nalut seeking to grab disputed land, prompting the GNC to issue a decision in December 2013 calling for the locals of Baten Al Jabal to return to their towns and villages and for land conflicts in the area to be resolved through the justice system.[10] While each of these cases is highly complex, arguably the most thorny internal displacement situation in Libya is the case of the Tawerghans. Focusing in particular on the Tawerghans, the "most obvious losers" of the revolution, the following sections highlight the living conditions and protection concerns facing Libyan IDPs and key obstacles to durable solutions to their displacement.[11]

A "Constant Nightmare": Daily Life and Protection Challenges for Libyan IDPs

Libya's four hundred thousand IDPs face innumerable challenges, most obviously the violence that caused their flight in the first place and continues to undermine their physical security in places of refuge. Libya's civil war, like the 2011 uprising before it, has subjected populated, residential areas to significant fighting, the use of heavy weapons, and indiscriminate shelling and bombardment. This not only poses a threat to existing IDPs, but also promises to generate more. The resulting destruction of many urban areas throughout Libya and the evictions that occurred after Gaddafi's fall have caused a severe housing crisis, leaving many Libyan IDPs to live in schools, unfinished administrative buildings, metal hangars, and parks, often with minimal access to clean water and heat. Many IDPs lack freedom of movement, with armed groups preventing them from fleeing or accessing badly needed food and medical supplies. The severe lack of medical supplies and competent care, compounded by looting, reduced imports due to the conflict, and the flight of foreign medical personnel, represents an additional set of intertwined challenges.[12]

The experience of displacement has been particularly harrowing for *azlam*-labeled communities. At best, perceived "loyalist" communities that were displaced during the revolution have been neglected; at worst, their uprooting has been followed by continued, systematic attacks intended to undermine both the possibility of return and their local integration elsewhere. This is the predicament befalling the Tawerghans, a group of sub-Saharan African descent who primarily lived in a town bearing the group's name, on the outskirts of Misrata.[13] The Tawerghans were perceived beneficiaries of the largesse of the Gaddafi regime, although Tawerghan IDPs suggest that the community reaped few tangible benefits from the former government, pointing to the lack of development projects and housing construction in their town before the revolution.[14]

Nevertheless, when the revolution broke out, various Tawerghan men fought with forces loyal to Gaddafi and participated in the siege on Misrata, which was characterized by brutal violence, including systematic rape. When the revolutionary forces gained the upper hand in the summer of 2011, forty-five thousand residents of Tawergha fled their homes in anticipation of a militia attack from Misrata.[15] This attack purposefully targeted and destroyed thousands of homes, businesses, and public buildings, leaving the town entirely deserted. The vast majority of Misratans remain vociferously opposed to the Tawerghans' return; after the initial siege, Misratan forces returned to Tawergha and destroyed even more of the town's infrastructure, with the aim of rendering the IDPs' dispossession complete and permanent. The purposeful expulsion of the Tawerghans and the denial of their right of return represent collective punishment for individuals' crimes and have been characterized by UN investigators and human rights groups such as Amnesty International and Human Rights Watch as crimes against humanity.[16]

After the destruction of their hometown, some Tawerghans fled the country.[17] Most, however, remain displaced within Libya, where life is, in the words of one IDP, a "constant nightmare" given the risks that come with their color and identity.[18] Indeed, "many Libyans believe race and class to be major factors that complicate the conflict. . . . Tawerghans are believed to have been enslaved in the past by Misratans. Misrata has traditionally been a major market and source of jobs for Tawerghans, and until the 2011 revolution many Tawerghans depended on Misrata for their jobs and livelihoods."[19] The IDPs have for the most part taken up residence in ill-serviced camps scattered across the country. Their collective punishment has not stopped with their expulsion. Rather, the camps have been subjected to attacks, including physical assaults, sexual and gender-based violence, and arson. Many such attacks have been perpetuated by militias looking to detain, interrogate, and torture Tawerghan men believed to have participated in the siege against Misrata. Tawerghan IDPs assert that the attacks against them are perpetrated not only by Misratan militias, but also by militias from other areas who seek to curry favor with the powerful Misratan groups.[20] According to Tawerghan IDPs who witnessed assailants arriving in government vehicles, these attacks have been perpetrated with state complicity, by actors who "hide behind the legitimacy of the state."[21]

The risk of attack has curtailed IDPs' freedom of movement. If they leave the camps, young men (who face particularly high risk of abduction) sometimes travel with elderly people and women (who are less likely to be targeted), but often for security reasons the men simply pass monotonous days inside the camps. Tawerghan local councils have pleaded with the Ministries of Defence and the Interior and the Office of Displaced People's Affairs in the Prime Minister's Office (PMO) to provide protection to the camps, but IDPs indicate that these pleas have been ignored. In the absence of government protection, the IDPs have organized themselves into shifts to watch over the camps, but continued raids against the camps make the limited nature of the protection provided by this informal system all too clear—a challenge that has only increased as violence has intensified with the outbreak of civil war.[22]

Insecurity and attacks by uncontrolled militias have also been major concerns for other displaced groups, including IDPs from Western Rayayneh.[23] Lack of knowledge about the fate of disappeared and incarcerated IDPs and the recognition that many have likely been tortured are sources of great distress, but the security situation hinders the ability of family members of missing or killed Tawerghans to raise their concerns with the government and seek redress.[24] As UNSMIL points out, such reprisals—particularly if they go without redress—risk generating long-term cycles of violence.[25]

In addition to physical insecurity, displacement has exposed Libyan IDPs to socioeconomic deprivations, including lack of access to housing and livelihoods, and has marginalized them from the post-Gaddafi government, fractured as it is. Tawerghan IDPs argue that owing to the powerful influence of Misratan officials, they have been "ostracized and blacklisted" when they try to approach or secure assistance from the government.[26] For example, some students have been unable to continue their studies because their files are being held in Misrata, while some Tawerghans have had their salaries withheld for the last four years.[27] IDPs also indicate that the former GNC member who was supposed to represent Tawergha did not effectively serve the population, stressing that he rarely visited the camps where the majority of Tawerghans live. Similarly, IDPs pointed to the lack of understanding of their concerns within the Office of Displaced People's Affairs, suggesting that staff working for this office should be recruited from the camps so that they can comprehend and "feel the suffering" of the displaced.[28] For their part, (former) PMO staff recognize that the government's efforts to negotiate solutions for different displaced groups on an ad hoc basis have met with limited success or have even been strongly opposed by displaced groups who accuse government actors of treason, and they suggest that formal decisions on displacement issues from the legislature can help to increase acceptance of particular courses of action, such as constructing new homes or addressing property disputes.[29] This prospect is now, however, rendered particularly difficult by the fractures emerging from the 2014 election and the ensuing violence.

Lackluster Responses and Barriers to Solutions

The Office of Displaced People's Affairs is charged with responsibility for Libyans displaced inside and outside the country. However, like other branches of the Libyan government, it has struggled to execute its mandate in light of the increased violence and political turmoil since the summer of 2014. Furthermore, this office and the government more broadly lack the requisite training and capacity to deal effectively with the displacement issue, and the relevant domestic legal and policy frameworks remain underdeveloped (despite several earlier internationally supported training initiatives). In particular, as staff working with the former PMO have argued, the continued practice by militias and other groups of displacing communities in order to grab their land needs to be clearly and explicitly banned under Libyan law.[30] At the same time, state commitment and capacity to enforce such laws needs to be strengthened if such legislative steps are to have any practical benefit—a prospect that remains far off as the government continues to be split between Tripoli and Tobruk.

From the perspective of the Tawerghans and other IDP communities, international responses to their plight have come primarily in the form of limited emergency assistance and efforts to record the violations committed against them, rather than through concrete support for preventing continued violations and enabling return or other durable solutions to their displacement. Although the UN Commission of Inquiry, for instance, explicitly detailed and condemned the "widespread and systematic" violence inflicted on the Tawerghan IDPs as a crime against humanity, some IDP leaders openly question the practical impact of such efforts.[31] Similarly, displaced Tuareg community leaders indicate that organizations such as Human Rights Watch and UNHCR have visited them and compared their situation to such cases as the former Yugoslavia and East Timor, highlighting the positive work that was done in these regions to advance justice and address displacement. However, in the words of one IDP leader, "We did not see their work on the ground [in Libya]"; these organizations "ask us to address and coordinate with the Libyan government. But the problem is the absence of viable government in Libya."[32]

The intentions of Libyan IDPs regarding the resolution of their displacement have not yet been systematically collected, although on the level of rhetoric the majority of Tawerghans and other IDPs are firmly committed to exercising their right to return to and rebuild their communities.[33] Some Tuareg IDPs, for example, have started settling into new communities in Awal but stress that this does not preclude their eventual return to Ghadamis. As a Tuareg IDP leader put it, "As for our return to Ghadamis, we consider it as a holy city, it is a spiritual city for Tuaregs that we cannot give up to anyone even if we are building something in the region of Awal. When the law of transitional justice is activated, we will not accept that others live in the city of Ghadamis. . . . [It] is our city, in which we have been living for thousands of years. We are the guardians of this region."[34]

Increasingly frustrated with their prolonged displacement and continued insecurity and abuse, Tawerghan IDPs threatened in early 2013 to undertake a unilateral return to their destroyed town, despite the retaliation such a move would undoubtedly provoke from Misrata. "We intend to go peacefully," a local leader indicated, "but if Misrata wants to kill us in order to stop our return, then they can go ahead. As things stand, we are already getting killed and detained."[35] The unilateral return was dissuaded in part by UNSMIL warnings that it could result in a massacre, but frustration continues to mount as community members feel that enabling their return is not on the government's agenda (even before the surge in violence since 2014), and the community has been subjected to repeated displacements from their camps.[36] While not explicitly denying return as an eventual option, the Libyan government has in the past suggested the construction of new shelters for the IDPs elsewhere in the country, an option many IDPs vociferously reject. Indeed, among the Tawerghans such suggestions have been met with particular mistrust as IDP community leaders believe that some of the prominent government officials who were advocating this option have roots or interests in Misrata.[37]

Beyond the general lack of security in Libya, one of the most prominent barriers to durable solutions for long-standing Libyan IDPs, particularly the Tawerghans, is the persistent assumption of communal culpability for violations committed during the revolution (despite the fact that the majority of the displaced were not involved, directly or indirectly, in perpetrating violence) and the perceived legitimacy of collective punishment. This problem has been greatly exacerbated by the state's inability and unwillingness to protect IDPs from such acts of retribution. Broadly, durable solutions for Libyan IDPs require the establishment of law and order, including an end to arbitrary arrests, the release of prisoners being held without charge, and the instigation of fair trials for those accused of violations. More particularly, enabling durable solutions for IDPs in situations that are becoming protracted requires overcoming assumptions of collective guilt and refuting preferences for collective punishment through awareness raising, dialogue, and accountability at the local and national levels. As discussed in greater detail below and as suggested by experiences in other countries struggling with the need to enable durable solutions to the displacement of populations potentially complicit in human rights violations, such processes can help to increase mutual understanding and recognition of past wrongs and how they may be effectively and fairly addressed.[38] The need for diverse forms of dialogue and awareness raising is reflected in the assertion of an IDP leader from Western Rayayneh who was pushing for his community to be able to return home but insisted that this must be done with "dignity": "If Zentan [the community whose members uprooted them] is asking us to apologize publicly and humiliate us in the process, then we don't want to return."[39] In August 2013, an agreement was reached between leaders from Western Rayayneh and Zentan allowing for the return of the displaced residents, and a reconciliation meeting to facilitate this process was held in October 2013 in a local mosque with elders, "wise men," and civil society representatives from both communities. While residents were reportedly satisfied with the agreement, in practice the return process has been limited by the need to rebuild homes that were massively damaged during the fighting. Local families lack the resources and the state lacks the capacity to complete this process promptly.[40]

Given that many of the victims and perpetrators of displacement have committed and endured a range of interlinked injustices, moving beyond "zero-sum game" conceptions of acknowledgment of and accountability for past wrongs will be essential to the eventual resolution of displacement and rebuilding of fractured communities across Libya. Of course, this is easier said than done, particularly in the absence of a breakthrough on the question of establishing security and promoting political reconciliation at the national level—a prospect that seems increasingly remote. As Haider Hasan, a member of Misrata's military council in Tripoli expressed it, "There is nothing to talk about regarding Tawergha and their war crimes in Misrata. Time is a great healer, and we should not talk about the problem now. Let the Tawerghans go wherever they want, but [there can be] no return to Tawergha."[41] Despite such perspectives, a "Reconciliation of Goodwill Committee" (Mussalahat El Kheir) was reportedly established by elders from Mirsata, but it did not succeed in satisfactorily addressing the problem from the perspective of either side.[42]

Further efforts have been discouraged by the fact that some of the few residents of Misrata who have spoken out against the fate of the Tawerghans have met with hostility and even extreme violence. For example, GNC member Hasan al-Amin questioned the abuse of the Tawerghans when he was appointed to Libya's human rights council but was subsequently pressured to apologize and left the GNC. A local sheikh, Mohammed Ben Othman, who spoke out about the Tawerghans' situation, was killed in 2012, allegedly for his stance on the issue.[43] At the national level, in August 2013 former prime minister Ali Zeidan proposed the instigation of reconciliation dialogues encompassing the question of displacement, but the suggestion was not well received. Indeed, the prime minister's suggestions "were immediately criticized, as some tribal groups claimed they had not been consulted. Since then, there has been little meaningful debate on the issue,"[44] particularly as new displacements caused by the violence in 2014 and 2015 have emerged. Were they eventually to take place, such dialogues would need to be predicated on increased understanding among former neighbors and among policymakers of IDPs' rights and obligations and why, for example, the arbitrary prohibition of their return is unacceptable from a human rights perspective.

Alongside the establishment of security at the local level, such dialogues may be essential precursors to addressing other barriers to return, such as the reconstruction of destroyed homes and infrastructure in Tawergha and elsewhere. However, using dialogue and accountability processes as a stepping-stone toward the resolution of the Tawerghans' displacement is particularly difficult because of the role of sexual and gender-based violence in the case. At the same time as they raise the legitimate argument that sexual violence cannot be blamed on the whole town, some Tawerghan IDPs problematically downplay the extent to which rape happened to Misratan women during the siege or seem to want to "neutralize" the Misratans' grievances by pointing out that some Tawerghan women were also subjected to rape. Others divert blame to members of Gaddafi's brigades (Kataeb) from across the country, who were also involved in the siege on Misrata.[45]

While a handful of Misratan leaders may be open to negotiating redress for the killings that occurred during the siege, they are generally unwilling to contemplate similar processes of dialogue and accountability regarding rape and other forms of sexual and gender-based violence. Libyan minister of justice Salah al-Marghani has argued that "Libyans' cultural heritage... can provide means of dealing with crimes such as murder or robbery, but not systematic rape. Accepting compensation for rape is a stigma. Even discussing rape is a source of embarrassment. Our legal system has regulations for how to deal with individual cases of rape, but not when a town is accused of rape by another town. Neither our legal nor our value systems can inform us what to do in this case."[46] This sense that the crime is beyond the scope of the legal and cultural framework leads to inaction: In the words of the justice minister, "We look at the problem, we acknowledge its existence, and then take no action to deal with it simply because we don't know how to deal with such a situation."[47]

According to Tawerghan leaders, the Libyan media has neglected or actively heightened negative perceptions of their community, perceptions they would like to have the opportunity to refute publicly as a step toward enabling their eventual return. In addition, they are seeking a formal apology that is televised or carried in Libyan newspapers.[48] In February 2013, Tawerghan leaders presented an apology to Misrata for the abuses that were undertaken by some Tawerghans; unsurprisingly, in light of the lack of prior dialogue and effective accountability systems, this apology was rejected. The eradication of trust between IDPs, particularly the Tawerghans, and other Libyans suggests that the international community has an important role to play not only in supporting a negotiated resolution to the civil war and tackling the dearth of security in the country, but also in encouraging dialogue and promoting durable solutions to displacement. This does not, however, discount the central role and responsibility of the Libyan state in the process. Indeed, while Libyans have historically never benefitted from an inclusive and responsive government, IDPs' expectations of the post-Gaddafi state are high: Despite their experiences since 2011, they continue to appeal to the state to take responsibility for assisting them, treating them as equal citizens, and enabling their return. It is time, they argue, for the victors of the revolution to turn from infighting to nation building, a move that requires increased attention to both the country's internal and cross-border displacement situations.[49]

Notes

1. Mitri, "Security Council Briefing"; IDMC, *Global Overview 2014*, 59.
2. Ibid., 6.
3. Chonghaile, Clar Ni, "Libyans Displaced by Civil Conflict Face Cruel Winter as Donor Funding Falls Short," *Guardian*, December 8, 2014, http://www.theguardian.com/global-development/2014/dec/08/libya-displacement-civil-war-cruel-winter-donor-funding-falls-short.
4. IDMC, "Libya: State Collapse," 6.
5. Ibid. For a map detailing the distribution of IDPs across Libya, see http://www.internal-displacement.org/middle-east-and-north-africa/libya/2015/libya-internal-displacement-as-of-march-2015.
6. Chonghaile, "Libyans Displaced."
7. Even before it had to pull out of Libya, UNHCR did not have a formal memorandum of understanding or framework agreement with the government of Libya, which limited its capacities and role.
8. While an agreement was reached in 2013 between Western Rayayneh and Zentan allowing for IDPs from Western Rayayneh to return to their homes, a similar agreement has not been concluded between Mashashya and Zentan. This has perpetuated the displacement situation and has reportedly exacerbated instability by prompting men from Mashashya to join the armed conflict.

9. Tuareg IDP civil society activist from Ghadamis, Libya, interview with the author, Tripoli, December 28, 2013.

10. Coordinator, Office of Displaced People's Affairs, Prime Minister's Office (at the time), interview with the author, Tripoli, Libya, December 22, 2013. For a helpful visual explanation of key events causing major internal displacement flows in Libya since 2011, see IMDC, "Libya State Collapse."

11. ILAC, *Rule of Law Assessment Report*, 32.

12. IDMC, "Libya: State Collapse," 7–9.

13. "Tawergha" is an Amazigh name. The area where the Tawerghans reside has been inhabited by black families of sub-Saharan African descent since the nineteenth century, when ancestors of contemporary Tawerghans were brought to the shores of Misrata as slaves and later enfranchised (although some claim that the Tawerghans ended up in the area due to the capsizing of a slave ship). Tawerghans remained reliant on Misrata for their basic needs, with many Tawerghans working in menial jobs in the city or enrolling in the army.

14. Head of Janzour IDP camp information center, interview with the author, Tripoli, Libya, January 6, 2013; Tawerghan IDP (1), supervisor of Al Fallah IDP camp, interview with the author, Tripoli, Libya, November 22, 2013. According to one Tawerghan IDP interviewed for this study, "Tawergha had historically been torn between its status as a Misrata suburb and its semiautonomy during [the] Gaddafi [regime].... The town suffered administrative injustice and abuse with only fifty housing units built since the king's era. Gaddafi did not even develop Tawergha." (Tawerghan IDP [3], interview with the author, Tripoli, Libya, November 22, 2013.) This interviewee went into exile in Tunisia in April 2014 following threats prompted by his denunciation in foreign media of random attacks against Tawerghans.

15. Some Libyan government officials have suggested that the Tawerghans left of their own accord. Under the Guiding Principles on Internal Displacement, those who flee in anticipation of an attack such as that levied on the town of Tawergha are to be considered IDPs. The actions taken by Misratan militias, with broad support from the Libyan government, to undermine the possibility of return and thus sustain the Tawerghans' displacement, are incontrovertible.

16. UN Human Rights Council, *Report of the International Commission*. The Tawerghans' predicament also represents a violation of the prohibition of arbitrary displacement, as articulated in Principle 6 of the Guiding Principles on Internal Displacement. Principle 6 indicates that displacement intended as collective punishment constitutes arbitrary displacement. See Williams, *Housing, Land and Property Issues*, 98.

17. Allegedly, some of those responsible for crimes committed against Misratans during the siege are among those who fled. Coordinator, Office of Displaced People's Affairs, interview. According to Tawerghan IDPs in Fallah refugee camp in Tripoli, some five thousand Tawerghans are in Egypt, where some are able to survive on salaries that they continue to receive from the government, while an

unknown number are in Tunisia. With the assistance of a German NGO, a small number of Tawerghans were able to obtain visas to leave for Germany. Tawerghan IDP (1), interview; Tawerghan IDP (3), interview.

18. Head of Janzour IDP camp information center, interview. Some interviewees suggested that the race dimension of the Tawerghan IDP situation has been overstated, while at the same time recognizing that historically racial equality and tensions have represented major challenges in Libya. (Coordinator, Office of Displaced People's Affairs, interview.) While Tawerghans are black, Misratans have their roots in Arab, Circassian, and Turkish ethnicities and have lighter skin.

19. Sharqieh, *Reconstructing Libya*, 21.

20. As a result of this dynamic, there is a sense among some Tawerghans that whether or not there is a sustained withdrawal of Misratan militias from Tripoli, this would not remove the dangers facing the IDPs.

21. Tawerghan IDP (3), interview. Researchers could not independently verify the accuracy of this claim.

22. Tawerghan IDP (1), interview; Tawerghan IDP (2), political activist, interview with the author, Fellah IDP camp, Tripoli, Libya, November 20, 2013; Tawerghan IDP (3), interview.

23. President of the reconciliation committee between al-Rayayna and al-Zentan, Nafusa Mountains, interview with the author, Western Rayaynah, Nafusa Mountains, Libya, January 19, 2013.

24. Head of Janzour IDP camp information center, interview; Tawerghan IDP (1), interview; Tawerghan IDP (2), interview; Tawerghan IDP (3), interview.

25. UNSMIL, "Transitional Justice."

26. Head of Janzour IDP camp information center, interview.

27. Tawerghan IDP (1), interview; Tawerghan IDP (2), interview; Tawerghan IDP (3), interview.

28. Ibid.

29. Coordinator, Office of Displaced People's Affairs, interview.

30. Ibid.

31. UN Human Rights Council, *Report of the International Commission*; head of Janzour IDP camp information center, interview; Tawerghan IDP (1), interview; Tawerghan IDP (2), interview; Tawerghan IDP (3), interview.

32. Tuareg IDP civil society activist from Ghadamis, interview.

33. In spite of strong rhetoric in support of return, discussions undertaken by PMO staff with Tawerghan IDPs suggest that some do not actually want to return, in part because some of their former neighbors committed violent crimes for which they have not been held accountable. Coordinator, Office of Displaced People's Affairs, interview.

34. Tuareg IDP civil society activist from Ghadamis, interview.

35. ICG, *Trial by Error*, 7.

36. Head of Janzour IDP camp information center, interview; Tawerghan IDP (1), interview; Tawerghan IDP (2), interview; Tawerghan IDP (3), interview.

37. Ibid.

38. See, for example, Phil Clark, "Bringing Them All Back Home: The Challenges of DDR and Transitional Justice in Contexts of Displacement in Rwanda and Uganda," *Journal of Refugee Studies* 27, no. 2 (2014): 234–57.

39. President of the reconciliation committee between al-Rayayna and al-Zentan, Nafousa Mountains, interview.

40. Ahmed Elumami, "Peace Deal between Reyayna and Zintan," *Libya Herald*, August 19, 2013, http://www.libyaherald.com/2013/08/19/peace-deal-between-zintan-and-reyayna/.

41. Sharqieh, *Reconstructing Libya*, 20.

42. Tawerghan IDP (1), interview; Tawerghan IDP (2), interview; Tawerghan IDP (3), interview.

43. Ibid.

44. Sharqieh, *Reconstructing Libya*, 30.

45. Head of Janzour IDP camp information center, interview.

46. Salah Marghani, Libyan justice minister (at the time), interview with the author, Tripoli, Libya, January 6, 2013.

47. Ibid.

48. Head of Janzour IDP camp information center, interview; Tawerghan IDP (1), interview; Tawerghan IDP (2), interview; Tawerghan IDP (3), interview.

49. Ibid.; Ben Guerdane, exiled former Libyan military officer, interview with the author, January 26, 2014.

3

Precarious Refuge

Displaced Libyans in North Africa

IN THE EARLY DAYS of the Libyan Revolution, hundreds of thousands of Libyans fled to neighboring countries to escape the violence. In Tunisia many stayed with friends or extended families, some rented hotel rooms and apartments, and others moved into temporary camps set up in the south of the country. Under long-standing arrangements between Libya and Tunisia, Libyans did not need a visa or any kind of formal status to enter Tunisia and stay for a period of up to three months. Under a 1973 convention between the two countries, Libyans are in theory allowed to freely move and work within Tunisia.[1] The ad hoc, temporary protection that was in effect granted to fleeing Libyans by the Tunisian authorities relieved some of the pressure on humanitarian agencies working to respond to other aspects of the Libyan crisis, such as the predicament of migrants displaced by the violence. Many Libyans who arrived in the initial period of the conflict overstayed this three-month limit, but, according to UNHCR, the Tunisian government was clear from the outset that given the crisis in Libya, it did not intend to take action to remove Libyans for having overstayed.[2]

After October 2011, many Libyans, particularly those who were supportive of the revolution, returned to Libya. Some with means moved fluidly between Tunisia and Libya, benefiting from the comparative stability in Tunisia.[3] At the same time, a significant group of Libyans remained or arrived in Tunisia and other neighboring countries for more prolonged and uncertain stays. While this population is diverse, many of these Libyans had—or are assumed to have had—ties to the fallen regime. Some were Gaddafi loyalists who fought actively against the revolution and were allegedly complicit in the regime's human rights violations. Others had much less direct connections to the prior regime but found that these connections were exaggerated in the context of postrevolution rivalries and power struggles. In some cases, the "connection" to the former regime is as tangential as having attended a rally or sold groceries to individuals in the Libyan armed forces.[4] Many are simply family members of suspected loyalists. Before seeking shelter in neighboring states, many were first internally displaced within Libya and now face increasing impoverishment in exile as their personal resources run dry. Some have resorted to begging in front of mosques in order to be able to pay for their children's school fees in Tunisia.[5] Fear is widespread among this population that their insecure status may eventually result in their forcible return to retributive violence, incarceration, and torture in Libya.[6]

This fear has only grown as more Libyans have poured into Tunisia following the upsurge in violence in 2014 and 2015, testing the limits of their neighbors' hospitality and tolerance. Focusing in particular on the situation in Tunisia, this chapter considers the plight of Libyans who fled across an international border, typically before the end of 2013 (that is, before the resurgent outflows in 2014 and 2015), but who generally have *not* sought or obtained formal protection under international refugee law. In the absence of secure status, many of these Libyans have attempted to remain "under the radar" in their host states, a situation that is becoming increasingly untenable as their displacement becomes more protracted and the risk of their entrenched marginalization grows. A rights-based response to their predicament is needed that combines enhanced protection against involuntary return with cross-border dialogue, reconciliation processes, and systematic, even-handed efforts to ensure accountability for involvement in serious violations of human rights. The development of such a rights-based response should be contextualized within broader processes of strengthening security, advancing transitional justice, and improving frameworks for responding to forced migration across North Africa.

Into the Shadows: Libyans' Search for Invisibility in Neighboring Countries

As the Libyan population in Tunisia and other neighboring countries has not been formally registered or surveyed, there are at present no conclusive estimates of its size or major demographic characteristics.⁷ Estimates of the Libyan population currently living in Tunisia and Egypt vary widely, with the number of Libyans in Tunisia ranging from five hundred thousand to 1.5 million, the latter figure quoted by the Tunisian minister of foreign affairs in August 2014. In April 2015, Tunisian officials estimated that there were one million Libyans living in Tunisia, equivalent to 10 percent of the Tunisian population. This population is predominantly made up of, according to one high-ranking Tunisian official, "middle class refugees," including those who have been in Tunisia since 2011 and more recent arrivals, but, in addition to those who are in need of protection who are unable to return to Libya, the population also includes Libyans who are simply visiting or working in Tunisia.⁸ While some Libyan government officials offer comparable figures, others question these estimates, suggesting that if these estimates were correct, the depopulation of Libyan communities would be more evident, as the Libyan population is only 6.2 million.⁹

Although there is a lack of data on the exiled population, it is clear that there is significant diversity within the diaspora. Libyans in neighboring states left the country for a range of reasons and have adopted different approaches to managing life in exile. Some, including former, low-ranking government workers, have only modest resources at their disposal.¹⁰ Others were senior officials actively working in support of the regime; some of these individuals are linked to the opposition to the government inside Libya and are supportive of efforts to foment instability in Libya.¹¹ While the size and characteristics of the Libyan diaspora is a difficult and sensitive issue to research, there is a clear need for more reliable data on the population in order to inform policymaking processes. Data is lacking not only on current conditions, but also on earlier return movements and the attitudes of exiled Libyans vis-à-vis an eventual return. Anecdotal evidence suggests that many are, in principle, interested in returning. However, since the initial wave of repatriation following the fall of the Gaddafi regime, returns have been very limited, and some of those who have returned have been the victims of revenge attacks.¹² Given the widespread violence in Libya, in late 2014 UNHCR issued a new position on returns to Libya, calling on all states to allow access for fleeing Libyans and "urg[ing] all states to suspend forcible returns."¹³

The Libyan government does not have a "formal position or policy regarding Libyans in Tunisia."¹⁴ However, as a Libyan government official expressed it, whatever "side" of the matter they find themselves on, "there is no Libyan family that has not been affected by this issue."¹⁵ Libyan government officials visiting Tunisia, including former president of the GNC Mohamed al-Magarief and former prime minister Ali Zeidan, have called for the diaspora to emerge from the shadows and return to Libya.[16] These calls have been received by exiles as "pointless," given the inability of the government (then and now) to protect would-be returnees from violence and ensure that those suspected of past wrongs receive a fair trial.[17] Exiles have also questioned the sincerity of such overtures, arguing that because the officials perceive them as Gaddafi loyalists, they "do not consider us human beings. We were forced out of our homes, and they do not want to see us return to our country."[18] Some Libyan government officials have met with exiled Libyans and also discussed the issue with their Tunisian counterparts. Significantly, the committee initially established in Libya under the NTC to address the issue of the Libyan diaspora in Tunisia was formed under the Ministry of Defense; this raised concerns on the Tunisian side as to why such an issue would be under the purview of the Ministry of Defense rather than the Ministry of Foreign Affairs, prompting the Tunisian government to refuse to engage with the committee. Later government démarches with the Tunisian government and the diaspora communities in Tunisia were undertaken by officials from the PMO, but Libyan officials came under domestic political pressure to stop such meetings with exiled groups.[19]

Although the presence of Libyans in Tunisia has become more prominent in Tunisian political debates since the arrival of thousands more Libyans in Tunisia in the summer of 2014, for the most part the issue is still not a heated feature of bilateral discussions, and the Tunisian public retains a largely welcoming attitude toward the Libyans. While there is a growing popular sense of "humanitarian fatigue," a public opinion survey conducted in March 2015 concluded that although 92 percent of Tunisians feel that the Libyan crisis poses risks for Tunisia (with two-thirds characterizing these risks as "enormous"), 67.5 percent say that the presence of Libyans in Tunisia poses no risk to the country.[20] When asked to identify two steps the Tunisian government could productively take to address the crisis, 72.1 percent indicated that the government should accept "refugees" from Libya. At the same time, 95.7 percent think the government must also pursue strengthened border control, reflecting widespread concern with smuggling and terrorism. Despite these strikingly welcoming attitudes (especially compared to the reluctance of Western states to accept asylum seekers), Tunisians are divided on the question of whether Libyan families should be integrated into Tunisian society, with 46.5 percent in favor of integration and 52.7 percent opposed.[21] Wary of shifting popular sentiments, some Libyan exiles have concluded that despite declining living standards and persistent fear of refoulement (forced return), their best chance for security is to remain "under the radar."[22]

Insecure Status, Lack of Documentation, and Fear of Return

The Libyan exiles' predicament can only be understood in its regional context. Movement between Libya and Tunisia in times of uncertainty is a historical feature of the relationship between the two countries. Both Tunisia and Egypt, the countries hosting the majority of the Libyan diaspora, are signatories to the 1951 Refugee Convention and the 1969 OAU Convention. Many of the displaced could potentially qualify for refugee status under one or both of these standards, as long as they have not, for example, committed crimes that would exclude them from recognition as refugees. The fact that the vast majority have not applied for formal refugee status is unsurprising given their ability to initially enter neighboring states without a visa and in light of the region's tradition of providing often generous hospitality to those who have fled their countries without determining formal refugee status. While this approach has effectively served many groups in need of shelter, it is arguably inadequate in this instance given the political sensitivities surrounding some of the Libyan exiles. Indeed, the main reason why most Libyans who have been in exile since 2011 have not sought out formal protective status is their fear that if they come to the attention of neighboring authorities, they may be deported, even if they have not in fact been complicit in past offenses—a reality that reflects lack of trust that the region's long traditions of hospitality will be sufficient to protect them in the face of rising political pressure, including from growing antiforeigner sentiment, particularly in Egypt.[23]

As the vast majority of Libyans in countries such as Tunisia and Egypt have not applied for refugee status, UNHCR offices in the region have had relatively little interaction with this population. UNHCR Tunisia staff indicate that they have had an "internal debate" about their role vis-à-vis Libyans in Tunisia who were linked to the former regime and are unable to return. Some at UNHCR have expressed the view that there is a need to open a dialogue with Tunisian authorities on the protection dimensions of the situation, recognizing that while starting such a conversation with Tunisian officials would be complicated by the diversity of perspectives on this issue within the Tunisian government, such a step would be important to ensure that, in accordance with respect for the principle of nonrefoulement, secure sanctuary is provided to those whose lives would be in danger if they were deported.[24] Conversations on the protection of displaced Libyans would also need to be situated as part of a broader effort to work with the government to strengthen its domestic asylum system and respond to other populations, including those forced from Syria, Mali, and the Central African Republic. In addition, such conversations would need to be cognizant of the possibility that some Libyans who were complicit in past abuses may be excluded from protection as refugees and of the need to follow the 1951 and 1969 conventions assiduously in order to preserve the credibility of the system.[25]

Despite the importance and complexity of the situation, UNHCR's engagement with the increasingly protracted exile population has been limited. UNHCR has focused instead on other priorities, such as the operation and closure of the Shousha refugee camp in June 2013 and helping to address the influx of Libyans into Tunisia in the summer of 2014 and over the course of 2015.[26] The lack of UNHCR engagement with the more long-standing Libyan population in Tunisia has arguably further exacerbated its marginalization and hindered the development of a more systematic, rights-based protection strategy. Yet, it is also reflective of the reluctance and fear of many members of the exile population to engage with any formal institutions, whether governmental or international.[27] In the words of one exiled Libyan, many forced migrants in Tunisia fear that Tunisian institutions and international organizations alike are "spying on them for the new Libyan regime," contributing to Libya's purported state-approved, militia-led "manhunt of forced migrants."[28]

As Tunisia allows Libyans to enter without a visa and remain for a period of up to three months, the exiles' initial arrival was relatively unproblematic. (Similarly, Libyans who have arrived in Tunisia since 2014 have also encountered relatively few initial obstacles.) Technically, Libyans who wish to stay longer in Tunisia need to apply for a residency permit or an extended-stay visa. Despite the assurances of Tunisian government officials that Libyans can obtain such permits, many exiles are not doing this, as they do not wish to draw attention to their presence in Tunisia and because they assume that this would require them to return to Libya and then reenter Tunisia, a prospect that is impossible for many of them.[29] Consequently, many exiles have come into an insecure immigration status that represents a source of deep unease.[30] Those who overstay are liable to pay a fine that is proportional to the amount of time they were in Tunisia without proper status, but many fear that the repercussions may be much more severe. An exile in the city of

Sousse captures the situation in this way: "It seems that the Tunisian authorities are turning a blind eye to the presence of forced Libyan migrants in Tunisian territory in relation to the duration of residence in the country when they overstay—which is contrary to the laws in force—and this is a good point. However, this remains an obsession for Libyan forced migrants. If the law is activated that would simply mean that they will be taken out to Libya" to face an "unknown fate."[31] Some exiles suggest that they would like to remedy their legal limbo by obtaining refugee status or another form of humanitarian protection.[32]

Many Libyans who fled to Tunisia, Egypt, and elsewhere have expired passports but are afraid to approach Libyan embassies or consulates to renew their documents, fearing that if they are identified, they may be tracked and subject to blackmail, harassment, or eventual deportation.[33] A 2014 decree from the Libyan Ministry of Foreign Affairs ratchets up the hurdles Libyan diaspora members face in obtaining updated documentation. Under this new policy, Libyans abroad must return to Libya to change their passports; Libyan embassies and consulates will no longer assist with this process.[34] Libyan diplomatic officials in Tunisia appear unwilling to take account of the risks and difficulties this policy presents for citizens in the diaspora, as reflected by the blunt assertion from the Libyan chargé d'affaires in Tunis that "those who overstayed in Tunisia must bear their responsibilities for their actions."[35]

Public statements from Libyan security officials and political leaders underscore their suspicion of the Libyan diaspora, exacerbating the exiles' fear of the fate they would meet if they were to return. In November 2012, for example, the commander of a branch of the Supreme Security Committee emphasized that the government is monitoring contacts between domestic opposition forces and exiled Gaddafi loyalists.[36] Even after Gaddafi's death, the "belief that former regime officials still are actively seeking to subvert the transition and causing security problems remains widespread."[37] According to the head of a prominent revolutionary brigade, intercepted phone calls confirm that loyalists in the diaspora were "actively plotting against the state"; it has been suggested that these loyalists, not Islamist militants, may have orchestrated the assault on the US consulate in Benghazi on September 11, 2012. Indeed, the day after the attack, former prime minister Abdulrahim al-Keeb declared in a press conference that "there is no doubt that Gaddafi loyalists are actively trying to undermine the country's stability."[38] While many regard the notion of Gaddafi loyalists regaining power in Libya as far-fetched if not paranoid, clashes between pro-Gaddafi loyalists and Libyan security forces and militias on the Tamanhint airbase in Sabha (southern Libya) and in the Wersheffana area of western Libya do raise concerns about exiles' continued intentions to undercut the new regime, exploiting growing dissatisfaction with the security situation and the poor performance and instability of the post-Gaddafi state.

Against the backdrop of the Libyan government's allegations of diaspora involvement in exacerbating instability and violence in Libya, high-profile extraditions have greatly increased many exiled Libyans' fear that as difficult economic conditions persist across North Africa and the push for prosecutions of alleged perpetrators in Libya grows, they too may become vulnerable to forced return.[39] Although only "a handful" of the more than eight thousand presumed Gaddafi loyalists held for alleged complicity in serious human rights violations were transferred from outside the country, these cases have been extensively debated.[40] They include the March 2013 extradition from Egypt to Libya of Qaddafi's cousin Ahmed Qaddaf el-Damm and his aides, the September 2012 extradition of former intelligence chief Abdullah al-Sanussi from Mauritania, and, perhaps most controversially, the June 2012 extradition of former Libyan prime minister Baghdadi Mahmoudi from Tunisia.

Described by one of his lawyers as an "historic farce," Mahmoudi's extradition process was requested by the Libyan government in 2011 after Mahmoudi entered Tunisia unofficially in the final days of the revolution. Mahmoudi applied for refugee status, a claim that UNHCR was requested to help determine and that the agency rejected in the first instance. UNHCR stressed to the Tunisian government that Mahmoudi did have a right to appeal this determination before being deported to Libya, but this was disregarded. Despite the opposition of the Tunisian president at the time, Foued Mebazzaa, the extradition order was signed by then–prime minister Hamadi Jebali, with the support of the interim Tunisian government, overturning the decision of Tunisia's own administrative courts. Allegations of torture emerged promptly upon Mahmoudi's transfer to Libyan custody, and concerns that Libya remains unable to guarantee a fair trial remain unresolved, particularly as Mahmoudi was among eight former high-level Gaddafi officials who received death sentences from a Tripoli-based court in July 2015.[41] The politically motivated nature of the extradition is widely recognized and has had negative repercussions for Tunisia's reputation for adherence to rule of law.[42] Mahmoudi's extradition stoked the fear of diaspora community members in Tunisia, who rationalized that if a former prime minister could be extradited, then "normal" Libyans in Tunisia would be entirely unprotected from a similar fate. In turn, this fear has reduced the willingness of many diaspora community members to contact or cooperate with official entities, whether Tunisian, Libyan, or international.

While the Mahmoudi case has left many exiles with an abiding fear that they too may be returned to torture in Libya, the Tunisian government appears to have reacted to the sustained criticism it received in relation to this case by largely resolving not to engage in further deportations of Libyan citizens, "turn[ing] a blind eye" to their lack of clear legal status in Tunisia, and keeping its borders open as more Libyans have sought shelter in Tunisia since the summer of 2014.[43] As expressed by the former Tunisian ambassador to Libya, Tunisia is a country known for its tolerance and has decided to tolerate the presence of Gaddafi loyalists and their families as long as they do not commit crimes and do not engage in corruption or money laundering. Admittedly, "there are people who try to sow trouble between both countries," and the Tunisian government has come under criticism from some quarters for refusing to engage in further deportations.[44] Perhaps in response to such criticisms, the Tunisian minister of foreign affairs confirmed in an August 2014 interview that the government had indeed deported some Libyans who "practiced politics in Tunisia."[45] However, the individuals who pose risks to smooth relations between Libya and Tunisia remain, in the Tunisian government's assessment, a minority. Security cooperation between Tunisia and Libya helps to identify individuals who may pose security concerns, but extraditions cannot, according to the ambassador, proceed on the basis of "rumors or unfounded allegations" and require the establishment of a functioning justice system in Libya.[46] These developments, particularly the inclusion of articles in the new Tunisian constitution protecting "political refugees" from expulsion, are laudable. Yet, in the absence of a comprehensive and consistently applied legal and policy framework governing the rights of noncitizens (including asylum seekers, refugees, and others who may be harmed upon returning to their country of origin), members of the Libyan diaspora in Tunisia remain vulnerable to a shift in the political tides that may heighten their risk of forced returns. If the security situation in Libya further declines, prompting increased flows of Libyans into an already resource-strapped Tunisia, such a turn may become increasingly likely.

Declining Living Conditions

Living under the radar is, as a Libyan activist and lawyer in Tunisia reflects, a double-edged sword: While exposure increases the exiles' perceived insecurity, living in the shadows exposes them to exploitation and entrenched marginalization.[47] Many exiled Libyans are experiencing declining socioeconomic conditions, as their personal resources are dwindling and have not been replaced with reliable access to livelihoods and services in neighboring states. At the same time, the presence of so many Libyans in Tunisia has had complex positive and negative economic ramifications for the host country and its citizens.

The influx of Libyans into Tunisia has reportedly resulted in increased rents and real estate prices in cities including Tunis, Sfax, Sousse, and Jerba, as well as increased costs for rents and hotel rooms in cities such as Gabes and Mahdia. Some business people have reaped significant benefits, with the presence of Libyans in Tunisia channeling an additional billion euros into the Tunisian economy by some estimates.[48] However, the increased prices have caused financial strains for Tunisians and poorer Libyans alike and generated tensions between locals and the exiles seen to be "invading" their neighborhoods—particularly since the renewed inflows in 2014 and 2015.[49] According to a 2015 public opinion survey, 64.3 percent of Tunisians believe the Libyan crisis has increased the cost of living in Tunisia, although many also recognize that it has brought benefits, including increased Libyan investments in Tunisia and revenue-generating visits to access medical services.[50] As Tunisian officials have stressed, the exiled Libyan population additionally places significant pressure on subsidized energy and food staples.[51]

Affording increased rents is a challenge for poor and working-class Tunisians, as well as for Libyans who have overstayed their legally allowed time in Tunisia. Some exiles have managed to meet their daily needs by working informally or relying on financial assistance from family members inside Libya or elsewhere in the diaspora. Others continue to receive salaries or other forms of financial support from the Libyan government, although many who were affiliated with the past regime or are assumed to have been complicit in past crimes have had their salaries suspended.[52] (As an advocate working with displaced Libyans in Tunisia points out, reinstating the provision of financial support to government employees who were not complicit in abuses could be an important step toward improving their standard of living in exile, rebuilding connections between the post-Gaddafi state and its displaced citizens and enabling their eventual return.[53]) However, many exiles lack access to remittances or viable livelihood opportunities, particularly given their lack of formal legal status, and were not government employees entitled to financial support from the state. Consequently, as a PMO staff member acknowledged, many "families ... who migrated abroad are in dire material economic need. They have exhausted their savings and therefore they are threatened in their residence abroad."[54] Economic desperation has reportedly increased exiles' vulnerability to human trafficking and has pushed some women to turn to dangerous coping strategies, including prostitution.[55]

While Libyan exiles in neighboring countries have not, for the most part, had reliable access to health care and schools, in a positive development the Tunisian government has implemented a series of ad hoc measures to address some of the needs of the diaspora population, particularly regarding access to education. Reportedly, the Tunisian government has decided to enable Libyan children in Tunisia to study for free in public schools. Some Libyan parents have still been reluctant to register their children, potentially because of concerns regarding their lack of formal status and their desire to avoid attracting the attention of governmental authorities. Others indicate that their reluctance to send their children to Tunisian schools stems from the concern that this will lead to their integration into Tunisian society and alleviate the pressure on the Libyan government to address their situation.[56] However, other Libyan parents have requested the Tunisian authorities to open new schools to teach Libyan children in Tunis, as well as in Sfax and Mahdia, where there are significant Libyan diaspora communities. Authorization was granted for some new schools to open, with Tunisian authorities facilitating the recruitment of teachers and overseeing pedagogy and curricula, in part to ensure that the education system is not used to foster hatred or extremism.[57]

While this policy may make a significant contribution to addressing a key challenge facing the exiled community, some exiles argue that it is local Tunisians who have been the main source of support for poorer exiled Libyans, suggesting that in contrast the "Tunisian government has been passive. It neither benefited us nor caused us damage, and we saw nothing from it."[58] Some Libyans have sought support from Tunisian charitable organizations, although their capacity is limited, particularly in light of the inflows since 2014. Some Tunisian civil society activists working with Libyan exiles suggest that beyond providing socioeconomic assistance, local and national civil society organizations have an important role to play in pressing the Tunisian state to develop stronger protection frameworks for noncitizens.[59] In addition to protection against refoulement, further support is needed, for example to ensure adequate access to health care and address physical security problems. Some Libyan exiles in Tunisia indicate that they enjoy a reasonable sense of physical security on a day-to-day basis, but at the same time reports circulate of alleged kidnappings and assassinations of Libyans there.⁶⁰ Some exiles have been subjected to threats that if they do not make blackmail payments, their whereabouts will be reported to the Tunisian Ministry of Justice and to Libyan authorities. Reportedly, an apolitical member of the Qadadfa tribe in Sirte who sought shelter in Tunisia was jailed when he did not respond to such threats.⁶¹ Like IDPs in Libya, many of those who have been displaced across borders lack freedom of movement, as their fear of being identified by the authorities compels them to limit their movements.⁶² Some trace their present insecurity to the NATO intervention, charging that the humanitarian implications of the uprisings and the subsequent intervention have been ignored, in part because they bring the wisdom and legitimacy of the intervention itself into further question. From the perspective of one former regime official, "Western intervention in Libya produced a new system in which human rights abuses have been practiced in an unprecedented way, making it possible to create an enormous security vacuum."⁶³

For many individuals and families, the culmination of these difficulties has exacted a considerable psychological toll. Many families are split between Libya and neighboring countries, reducing access to typical support structures and increasing psychological strain, particularly given fears for the safety of family members remaining in Libya.⁶⁴ Libyans in exile have in some instances tried to manage the challenges they face by coming together to hold meetings, discuss their problems, and extend support to one another, including financially.⁶⁵ However, the experiences of other groups of undocumented forced migrants suggests that in the longer term, lack of legal status, political voice, and socioeconomic security can foster new grievances and create conditions for the flourishing of criminal networks, as members of undocumented communities cannot generally appeal to the government or the police for assistance when they encounter problems.⁶⁶ Defusing these risks by extending rights-based protection and assistance to Libyan exiles (and eventually promoting access to durable solutions) is undoubtedly in the interests not only of the displaced themselves, but also the Tunisian and Libyan states and societies more generally.

Dismantling an "Army of Opposition," Advancing Durable Solutions

Libyan exiles are close observers of the evolving situation in Libya and draw direct connections between their predicament and the inability of internally displaced Tawerghans, Ghuwalish, and Werfella to return to their hometowns.[67] Reflecting on the ongoing violence and the challenge of resolving Libya's displacement situation, an exile in Zarzis suggests that "the main thing for us is to free prisoners and bring internally displaced Libyans like Tawerghans back to their towns. This is even more important than our return."[68] Another exile asks, "As long as internally displaced Libyans cannot find peace, how do you expect it for us living outside Libya?"[69]

Just as the resolution of Libya's internal displacement situation is a long-term challenge, so too is the pursuit of durable solutions for those displaced across borders. Yet, the long-term nature of the challenge cannot serve as an excuse for inaction: The perpetuation of a marginalized exile population in neighboring countries risks creating, in the words of the first post-Gaddafi minister of health, a potential "army of opposition."[70] The longer this population is forced to remain in exile, the more difficult it may become to enable the exiles' return and address the grievances dividing them and their conationals.[71]

Part of the challenge surrounding the development and implementation of a rights-based approach to displaced Libyans in Tunisia is that while the *IASC Framework on Durable Solutions for Internally Displaced Persons* provides consolidated guidance on supporting the resolution of internal displacement situations, there is no equivalent, consolidated framework for supporting durable solutions for populations such as the Libyan diaspora in Tunisia and Egypt, who lack formal refugee status but are unable to return to their country or effectively integrate into their country of residence. Even in the absence of a clear framework to inform the resolution of displacement, some Libyan exiles have attempted to carve out their own durable solutions: Well-resourced families have left Tunisia to go to Morocco or Egypt or have applied for immigration to Europe, while others have purchased residency papers for Tunisia and do not intend to return to Libya.[72] But these options are out of reach for the sizable proportion of the Libyan diaspora population who remain in neighboring states with dwindling resources and insecure status, struggling to simply sustain their situation of limbo—a challenge exacerbated by the lack of international attention to this issue, leaving displaced Libyans ripe for abuse and without recourse for rights violations.

Further challenges derive from the fact that the Tunisian government itself is quite new and lacks extensive experience dealing with refugee and displacement situations.[73] Tunisia has a duty to develop laws, policies, and administrative systems to address the rights and well-being of noncitizens in Tunisia, building on the inclusion of the right to political asylum and the prohibition of the refoulement of "political refugees" in the new Tunisian constitution passed on January 27, 2014, and the important steps taken to increase access to education for Libyan children in Tunisia.[74] UNHCR has expressed its intention to support the return and reintegration of Libyan refugees in the region when the conditions are appropriate, an engagement that could potentially be shaped so that it also benefits those without formal refugee status but with similar protection concerns. The UN refugee agency could potentially also play a significant role in strengthening the capacity of the Tunisian and Libyan governments to increase access to durable solutions.[75] This, of course, depends on the restoration of increased stability in Libya, a task that is well beyond the capacities of humanitarian agencies.

While the Tunisian government is presently broadly—and commendably—committed to protecting exiled Libyans from forced returns, some Libyan officials anticipate that if host states' political incentives shift, they may begin to push returns. For this reason, in 2013 the Libyan Office of Displaced People's Affairs presented a draft framework to the Tunisian and Egyptian governments on this issue. However, Libya's neighbors refused to engage in discussion of such a framework, a decision Libyan officials attributed to their neighbors' desire to retain a "political and economic pressure card."[76] The potentially tenuous nature of the support Tunisia is extending to Libyan exiles is reflected in an August 2014 interview with former Tunisian minister of foreign affairs Mongi Hamdi, who indicated that "today, there are more than 1.5 million Libyan citizens in Tunisia and no other country has hosted such a large number of Libyans. We support them in the same way we support Tunisian citizens. They go to public Tunisian schools and they are treated in Tunisian public hospitals. They consume subsidized basic items like the Tunisians and we have stood by their side without complaining." However, he pointed out, "Under the current economic conditions, it is difficult for Tunisia to host more Libyans. . . . They are in our hearts, but we are keen to maintain the stability of our country and we do not accept anyone tampering with the country's security."[77]

Civil society organizations in Libya, as well as in Tunisia and other neighboring states, also have important roles to play in strengthening protection for displaced Libyans and increasing access to durable solutions. These organizations need to be more systematically supported and engaged.[78] Civil society organizations have particularly important roles to play in laying the groundwork for the eventual resolution of the displacement situation by encouraging more balanced media coverage of the problem, showing the diversity of the displaced population and why resolution of the displacement situation is in Libyans' collective interests. They also have important roles to play in proactively providing human rights education to Libyans at home and in the diaspora.[79] As a Libyan exile in Tunisia points out, the displaced themselves have important roles to play in overcoming their fears and raising their voices with civil society organizations, as well as international agencies such as UNHCR and IOM that can help to raise awareness of their concerns and support solutions for them.[80] An even greater challenge is to move beyond thinking in the binary terms of "pre-" and "post-" Gaddafi. As a PMO official responsible for Libyan IDPs and exiles expressed it, the challenge is for exiled Libyans to "change their rhetoric and stop thinking about revenge and pointing to the negativity of the Libyan Revolution and its supporters. This is it: Gaddafi died, the former regime has been defeated, the rhetoric has to change in order to reach an intersection between the two parties and extend the hand of brotherhood."[81] In the PMO's conversations with exiled Libyans, there was some support for this perspective, bearing in mind that in many ways the challenge is the same for the "victors" of the revolution and other parties now engaged in a vicious civil war: to move beyond revenge and self-interested power struggles and address the instability wracking Libya by developing a shared and sufficiently accommodating vision for the country's future.

As it stands, very few Libyans who fled the country in order to escape retaliatory violence are known to have voluntarily returned; instead, the ranks of Libyans in Tunisia have swelled with new arrivals since 2014. Little is known about the conditions the limited number of returnees face, although it is suggested that they are rarely able to go back to their home communities.[82] Some exiles who have maintained contact with returnees indicate that they "live in constant fear that at any time, militias may storm in. There is no safety or stability in their lives."[83] The Department of Displaced and Forced Migrants' Affairs corroborated this assessment, pointing, for example, to the experience of a group of five exiles who returned to Libya in secret and attempted to establish themselves in new communities but found that within six months of returning they were rounded up by militia forces, incarcerated, and tortured. Upon their release, they fled back to Tunisia.[84] Such experiences, alongside the circulation of photos of tortured prisoners and the more general upsurge in violence, have strengthened the conviction among many Libyans in the diaspora in Tunisia and elsewhere that they cannot return and that the forced migration of former Gaddafi supporters as a mass punishment has been rendered a fait accompli.[85]

Despite such experiences, some members of the Libyan government have insisted that it is up to Libyans in neighboring countries to return if they wish, disingenuously suggesting that those who were not involved in past crimes, including children and families of former regime officials, will not be questioned or harassed.[86] Other government officials, including the minister of justice, more frankly recognize that the perpetuation of cross-border displacement is fueled not only by fear of the consequences the state may compel them to bear for their past actions, but even more so by a fear of the consequences of the state's lack of capacity—and in some quarters, lack of willingness—to control armed groups bent on exacting revenge. This concern has only grown with the rise of competing governments in Tobruk and Tripoli. As the minister of justice indicates, the "displaced don't fear the law and the possibility of being tried" as much as they "genuinely fear returning to a lawless country where torture is widespread. . . . When there is a state of law, their problems will be resolved. Solving the displacement problem is done through solving the security problem."[87] This assessment is echoed by some exiled Libyans, such as a former member of Gaddafi's personal security detail who fled to Tunisia and who states, "We are not afraid of being prosecuted and being held accountable. We demand it for every person," but adds, "In the current situation, we will be prosecuted by these militias. If we suppose that there is transitional justice in Libya, I am ready to be held accountable."[88]

Alongside strengthening the state's capacity to prevent vigilantism, enabling future returns will depend on eventually developing and publicly explaining a prosecutorial strategy that ensures that those responsible for major violations will be held accountable and that provides clarity on approaches to accountability and reconciliation involving individuals whose association with the former regime was on a much lower level. As a modest step toward reframing the relationship between the displaced and the post-Gaddafi state, setting the stage for an eventual return, a Libyan reconciliation activist working in Tunisia suggests that the Libyan government, through its embassy in Tunisia, provide monthly payments to needy diaspora members (recognizing that despite the chaos in Libya, thousands of exiled Libyans continue to receive regular payments from the Libyan government, which many rely on for their subsistence). Such a modest step could, if accompanied by improved stability and security assurances, gradually encourage a sense of belonging and acceptance in the post-Gaddafi state.[89]

Ultimately, the continued internal and external displacement of Libyans is reflective of the failure to establish a viable state in the wake of the revolution and could perpetuate state-building failures by exacerbating uncertainty and instability.[90] It is assuredly in the interests of post-Gaddafi Libya and its neighbors to address this issue, foreclosing the possibility that a generation of children may be brought up on the margins of society, with grievance as a defining characteristic of their identities.[91] Even though the possibility of a large-scale return of Libyans from neighboring countries is slight in the near future, it is important to plan for eventual returns, including by setting the stage to effectively and fairly address questions such as property claims that almost inevitably accompany return processes.

As with the internally displaced population of Libya, achieving durable solutions for Libyan forced migrants in neighboring states depends first and foremost on meeting interrelated challenges: the establishment of security, the negotiated resolution of the current conflict, and the instigation of dialogue and even-handed transitional justice processes—hurdles addressed in more detail in the concluding chapter.

Notes

1. Omer Karasapan, "The Impact of Libyan Middle-Class Refugees in Tunisia," Brookings Institution Future Developments (blog), March 17, 2015, http://www.brookings.edu/blogs/future-development/posts/2015/03/17-libyan-refugees-tunisia-karasapan.

2. Three UNHCR Tunisia staff members, interviews with the author, Tunis, Tunisia, January 17, 2014.

3. Ibid.

4. Marine Olivesi, "These Libyan Refugees Feel Trapped in Tunisia, and There's Not Much They Can Do about It," Public Radio International, May 20, 2014, http://www.pri.org/stories/2014-05-20/these-libyan-refugees-feel-trapped-tunisia-and-theres-not-much-they-can-do-about.

5. Mohamed Mokhtar, "The Costliest Privilege," Correspondents.org, June 12, 2014, http://www.correspondents.org/node/5396.

6. Gaddafi loyalist (1), interview with the author, Zarzis, Tunisia, February 10, 2014; Gaddafi loyalist (2), interview with the author, Zarzis, Tunisia, February 10, 2014; Gaddafi loyalist (3), interview with the author, Zarzis, Tunisia, February 10, 2014; Gaddafi loyalist (4), interview with the author, Zarzis, Tunisia, February 10, 2014; Tuareg IDP civil society activist from Ghadamis, interview; A. M., exiled Libyan former senior internal security official, interview with the author, Sousse, Tunisia, 2014; M. T., exiled Libyan former bodyguard to Gaddafi, interview with the author, Zarzis, Tunisia, 2014.

7. The qualitative data gathered through this study is indicative of the range of challenges faced but cannot be taken as representative.

8. Mongi Hamdi, "We Must Protect Our Borders," interview by Hasan al-Ayadi, Correspondents.org, August 28, 2014, www.correspondents.org/node/5701; Ridha Boukadi, Tunisian ambassador to Libya, interview with the author, Tripoli, Libya, December 16, 2013; Brookings Institution, "Overlooked Crisis."

9. Coordinator, Office of Displaced People's Affairs, interview. The Libyan chargé d'affaires in Tunisia estimated that by the winter of 2014, there were some 400,000 to 500,000 Libyan exiles in Tunisia but also floated the figure of 750,000, stressing that not all Libyans in Tunisia have political or other concerns that would infringe upon their ability to return to Libya without difficulty. Libyan chargé d'affaires, interview with the author, Tunis, Tunisia, February 12, 2014.

10. Misratan officials have encouraged the prosecution of low-ranking government workers such as cooks, drivers, and accountants if they worked for Gaddafi's security officials. See ICG, *Trial by Error*, 35. This may have encouraged the flight of these working-class former government employees.

11. Libyan reconciliation activist, interview with the author, Tunis, Tunisia, May 2013.

12. Ibid.; Libyan chargé d'affaires, interview; Gaddafi loyalist (1), interview; Gaddafi loyalist (2), interview; Gaddafi loyalist (3), interview; Gaddafi loyalist (4), interview.

13. UNHCR, *UNHCR Position on Returns to Libya* (Geneva: UNHCR, 2014).

14. Libyan chargé d'affaires, interview.

15. Coordinator, Office of Displaced People's Affairs, interview.

16. Libyan chargé d'affaires, interview.

17. A. M., interview.

18. Gaddafi loyalist (3), interview.

19. Boukadi, interview.

20. Brookings Institution, "Overlooked Crisis"; Konrad-Adenauer-Stiftung and Sigma Conseil, *Les répercussions de la crise Libyenne sur la Tunisie* (Tunis: Konrad-Adenauer-Stiftung and Sigma Conseil, 2015), http://www.kas.de/wf/doc/kas_40808-1522-3-30.pdf?150504164905.

21. Konrad-Adenauer-Stiftung and Conseil Sigma, *Les répercussions de la crise Libyenne*. At a public event on the Libyan displacement crisis at the Brookings Institution in April 2015, the Tunisian ambassador to the United States suggested that Tunisians' hesitancy to promote the integration of Libyans may be tied in part to their reluctance to give up hope for the stabilization and reconstruction of Libya, a long-standing and important economic partner for Tunisia. See Brookings Institution, "Overlooked Crisis."

22. Coordinator, Office of Displaced People's Affairs, interview. In a potentially troubling incident, UNHCR received a delegation of Libyan officials in 2013 who were looking into the situation of Libyans in Tunisia. Some came with lists of names from the Libyan Ministry of Education that they sought to verify with UNHCR, in the context of the preparation of a report on Libyan children in Tuni-

sia that was purportedly being undertaken as part of an effort to promote national reconciliation. UNHCR lacks such detailed information on Libyans in Tunisia and would not in any event share such information with country-of-origin officials. (Three UNHCR Tunisia staff members, interviews.) If this was not simply a pretext for attempting to gather personal information on Libyans resident in Tunisia, Libyan government officials should be aware that soliciting such data in this manner is clearly not conducive to fostering trust and eventually reconciliation between the government and citizens in the diaspora.

23. Conducting research on a population that often endeavors to remain unnoticed raises a range of ethical concerns, in light of which we have removed all details that may be used to identify our Libyan interviewees in Tunisia. In deciding to draw attention to the need for a rights-based response to this group, we were motivated by recognition of the negative socioeconomic and psychological implications of protracted limbo for populations with insecure migration status and by the risk of unilateral or unregulated deportations that noncitizens face in many regions of the world, including the Middle East and North Africa. In Saudi Arabia, for example, over the course of 2013 and 2014, hundreds of thousands of noncitizens were rapidly deported, some to deeply insecure circumstances, with barely any recognition or push-back from international actors. Publicly recognizing the challenges faced by many members of the Libyan population in Tunisia is a first step toward ensuring that with a change of political environment they do not find themselves exposed to a similar fate.

24. The cardinal principle of the international refugee regime, the commitment to nonrefoulement entails that states will not return any individual to a territory where he or she faces a well-founded fear of persecution or risks being arbitrarily deprived of life or subjected to major human rights violations. See Guy Goodwin-Gill and Jane McAdams, *The Refugee in International Law*, 3rd ed. (Oxford: Oxford University Press, 2007), chap. 5.

25. Three UNHCR Tunisia staff members, interviews.

26. Ibid. There was a diversity of perspectives among UNHCR staff interviewed for this study regarding the extent to which the agency has an accurate profile of the Libyan diaspora population, protection concerns they face in neighboring countries, and UNHCR's potential role and responsibilities vis-à-vis members of this population who fear for their well-being if they were to return to Libya. UNHCR did issue initial guidance on the outflow into Libya. See UNHCR, "Protection Considerations with Regard to People Fleeing from Libya: UNHCR's Recommendations," UNHCR, March 29, 2011, http://www.unhcr.org/4d67fab26.html, as well as the updated UNHCR position on returns to Libya in November 2014, http://www.refworld.org/pdfid/54646a494.pdf.

27. Coordinator, Office of Displaced People's Affairs, interview; Béchir Essid, Tunisian lawyer defending displaced Libyans abroad and president of a committee with the same name, interview with the author, Tunis, Tunisia, January 25, 2014.

UNHCR staff in Tunisia indicate that the office has not encouraged Libyans in Tunisia to approach the UNHCR office to register as asylum seekers. Some of the few Libyans who have approached the agency indicated that the only support they would be interested in receiving from it would be assistance to leave the country, which, in some isolated cases, it has provided. For instance, the office helped a former Ministry of Foreign Affairs official to secure a visa for a European country. Three UNHCR Tunisia staff members, interviews.

28. A. M., interview.

29. Gaddafi loyalist (1), interview; Gaddafi loyalist (2), interview; Gaddafi loyalist (3), interview; Gaddafi loyalist (4), interview.

30. Lack of secure immigration status is a particular concern for families who have not been able to register the birth of new children. Libyan reconciliation activist, interview; Essid, interview.

31. A. M., interview.

32. Ibid.

33. Libyan reconciliation activist, interview; three UNHCR Tunisia staff members, interviews; Essid, interview; Boukadi, interview; A. M., interview.

34. Essid, interview; "Mana' 'istikhraj wa tajdid jawaz al-safar al-Libi bil-kharij" [Ban on issuance or renewal of Libyan passport abroad], Libyens.net (blog), January 22, 2014, http://tinyurl.com/n4hnsbx . In January 2014, the chairman of the Libyan Passports and Nationality Authority gave instructions to stop the issuance and renewal of the old green passport used in the Gaddafi period. The decision took effect on January 21, 2014, and made it mandatory for any Libyan citizen wishing to obtain the new blue passport to return to Libya in order to do so.

35. Libyan chargé d'affaires, interview.

36. ICG, *Trial by Error*, 22.

37. Ibid., 29; Libyan reconciliation activist, interview.

38. ICG, *Trial by Error*, 29.

39. Libyan activist and lawyer, interview with the author, Tunis, Tunisia, May 2013.

40. ILAC, *Rule of Law Assessment Report*, 34.

41. "Tunisia: Extradition of Former Libyan Prime Minister Violates Human Rights," Amnesty International, June 25, 2012, http://www.amnesty.ca/news/news-item/tunisia-extradition-of-former-libyan-prime-minister-violates-human-rights; Kirkpatrick, "Son of Muammar el-Qaddafi Sentenced to Death"; "Libya Trial: Gaddafi Son Sentenced to Death." One of Mahmoudi's lawyers, Mabrouk Khourchid, stated to the press on August 3, 2015, that the committee for the defense of Gaddafi's last prime minister intended to pursue Tunisian officials from the former Tunisian Islamist-led government, including former prime minister Hamadi Jebali and former president Moncef Marzouki, for having extradited Mahmoudi to Libya, well knowing that his life would be threatened. Officials from the Ennahdha party defended the decision by stating that they obtained guarantees

from the Tripoli authorities that Mahmoudi would receive fair treatment and a fair trial and that Mahmoudi lost his appeal in a Tunis court to stay in Tunisia. In addition to Mahmoudi, death sentences were also brought down for Gaddafi's son, Saif al-Islam Gaddafi, and former intelligence chief Abdullah al-Sanussi, who was returned to Libya from Mauritania, reportedly after a payment of $200 million to secure the extradition. (Mahmoudi was allegedly also returned for a payment of $200 million.) The defendants reportedly had little or no access to lawyers. At the time of the trial, Saif al-Islam, also wanted by ICC, was held by Zentani militias who do not recognize the authority or legitimacy of the Tripoli court and refused to hand him over for punishment.

42. Essid, interview; Libyan chargé d'affaires, interview.
43. Essid, interview.
44. Boukadi, interview.
45. Hamdi, "We Must Protect Our Borders."
46. Boukadi, interview.
47. Libyan activist and lawyer, interview.
48. Karasapan, "Impact of Libyan Middle-Class Refugees."
49. Moez Jamai, "Refugees or Tourists?," Correspondents.org, August 22, 2014, www.correspondents.org/node/5678; Libyan chargé d'affaires, interview; Lotfi Azzouz, director, Amnesty International Tunisia, interview with the author, Tunis, Tunisia, 2014. Some wealthy Libyan exiles have purchased homes in Tunisia, although this is not an option for the considerable proportion of the population who come from more modest backgrounds.
50. Konrad-Adenauer-Stiftung and Sigma Conseil, *Les répercussions de la crise Libyenne*.
51. Karasapan, "Impact of Libyan Middle-Class Refugees"; Brookings Institution, "Overlooked Crisis."
52. Boukadi, interview; M. T., interview.
53. Essid, interview.
54. Coordinator, Office of Displaced People's Affairs, interview.
55. Libyan reconciliation activist, interview; Dr. Fatma Hamroush, former Libyan minister of health and reconciliation activist, interview with the author, Dublin, February 2014; Coordinator, Office of Displaced People's Affairs, interview.
56. Coordinator, Office of Displaced People's Affairs, interview.
57. Boukadi, interview.
58. M. T., interview.
59. Essid, interview; A.M., interview; Azzouz, interview.
60. Gaddafi loyalist (1), interview; Gaddafi loyalist (2), interview; Gaddafi loyalist (3), interview; Gaddafi loyalist (4), interview.
61. Essid, interview.
62. Ibid.
63. Ibid., A. M., interview.

64. Coordinator, Office of Displaced People's Affairs, interview; Gaddafi loyalist (1), interview; Gaddafi loyalist (2), interview; Gaddafi loyalist (3), interview; Gaddafi loyalist (4), interview.

65. Libyan reconciliation activist, interview.

66. See, for example, Megan Bradley, "Unlocking Protracted Displacement: Central America's 'Success Story' Reconsidered," *Refugee Survey Quarterly* 30, no. 4 (2011): 84–121, for a discussion of this dynamic as it relates to the insecurity faced by undocumented Central Americans in the United States and the rise of transnational gangs such as Mara Salvatrucha.

67. A. M., interview; M. T., interview; Gaddafi loyalist (2), interview.

68. Gaddafi loyalist (2), interview.

69. M. T., interview.

70. Hamroush, interview. Dr. Hamroush's father was arrested and jailed for four years under Gaddafi, prompting her to work actively against the regime and assume a leadership position in the post-Gaddafi government. Although her own family was victimized by the previous regime, she has taken a leading role in encouraging dialogue and reconciliation with exiled loyalists, pragmatically recognizing that disaffected citizens will work against the new government unless they are given incentives not to do so.

71. Ibid.

72. Libyan reconciliation activist, interview.

73. Essid, interview.

74. Azzouz, interview. Article 26 of the Tunisian constitution indicates that "the right to political asylum shall be guaranteed as prescribed by law. Surrendering political refugees shall be prohibited." Tunisian law also prohibits the return of noncitizens who may be face torture, even if they are not "political refugees."

75. UNHCR, *Global Appeal 2012–2013*, 134.

76. Coordinator, Office of Displaced People's Affairs, interview.

77. Hamdi, "We Must Protect Our Borders."

78. Marghani, interview.

79. Coordinator, Office of Displaced People's Affairs, interview; A. M., interview.

80. A. M., interview.

81. Coordinator, Office of Displaced People's Affairs, interview.

82. Ibid.; Gaddafi loyalist (1), interview; Gaddafi loyalist (2), interview; Gaddafi loyalist (3), interview; Gaddafi loyalist (4), interview.

83. M. T., interview.

84. Coordinator, Office of Displaced People's Affairs, interview; Essid, interview.

85. Libyan activist and lawyer, interview.

86. Libyan chargé d'affaires, interview; Suleiman Awad al-Zouli, GNC member and chairman of GNC Legislative and Constitutional Affairs Committee, interview with the author, Dublin, Ireland, February 2014.

87. Marghani, interview.
88. M. T., interview.
89. Libyan reconciliation activist, interview. A similar proposal was made by a powerful military council in Tripoli, which suggested that the Libyan government pay Libyan families in Tunisia $500 a month to ensure "they live in dignity and don't resort to illegal work." A council member argued that "they are Libyans after all, and we should not accept that Libyans live in the streets of Tunisia."
90. Coordinator, Office of Displaced People's Affairs, interview.
91. Libyan reconciliation activist, interview. On the involvement of aggrieved diaspora populations in conflict, see, for example, Huma Haider, "Transnational Transitional Justice and Reconciliation: The Participation of Conflict-Generated Diaspora in Addressing the Legacies of Mass Violence," *Journal of Refugee Studies* 27, no. 2 (2014): 207–33.

4

Durable Solutions

Obstacles and Prospects

IN LIGHT OF LIBYA's "political chaos and ongoing conflict, durable solutions appear ever more remote."[1] Given the profound impact of the civil war on Libya's already serious displacement situation, it is clear that a new strategy is urgently needed to manage the crisis until the war is over and comprehensive support for durable solutions can be implemented. To be sure, the authority of the state in Libya has been severely compromised as a result of the militias' fighting. However, the state is still capable of developing improved strategies to deal with the current crisis, and measures that could help the displaced are still within its own reach. The state should seriously increase investments in shelter for the internally displaced. In the near absence of the state, civil society organizations, local councils, and international organizations (working remotely through local partners) have attempted to assist IDPs, in particular those affected by the current war, such as in the town of Kikla. Nevertheless, the capacity of these groups remains limited, meaning that current needs will go unmet without increased state support. Despite its weakness, the state can and should also increase its provision of other forms of humanitarian assistance, including cash transfers, whether directly or through partners. The Libyan state's struggles to perform its basic functions in the face of a civil war and the emergence of competing parliaments are significant, but supporting IDPs remains a core responsibility of the state, even if it has to be executed in collaboration with international organizations and NGOs. Strategic humanitarian assistance can prevent the crisis from worsening and the displaced from seeking alternative and potentially risky avenues for supporting themselves.

Notwithstanding the importance of developing and implementing an enhanced strategy to manage the pressing current concerns raised by the displacement crisis, this chapter offers some additional reflections on key issues that must be considered in the context of planning for the eventual pursuit of durable solutions for Libyan IDPs and exiles. These issues include the establishment of security and rule of law, the participation of displaced populations in negotiation and dialogue processes, and the role of transitional justice and reconciliation processes in supporting durable solutions.

The Lynchpin: Security and Rule of Law

Security is, in the words of one Libyan government official, the "first and main barrier to return."[2] "As long as Libyan authorities are unable to rein in these militias," a representative of Amnesty International in Tunisia argues, "there is no guarantee that if these Libyans go home they will be safe and get a fair trial" or be able to benefit from a minimum level of physical security as they go about their daily lives.[3] The extent of the upheaval in Libya, including attacks on high-profile targets and individuals, leaves would-be returnees fearful that their security concerns will not be addressed. As a Libyan exile in Zarzis expressed it, "When you see that the prime minister was abducted, do you think they will find a solution for me?"[4] Another exile offered an even blunter assessment: In the current circumstances, returning to Libya would be "like signing my death sentence."[5]

Arguably, the escalating instability in Libya, particularly over the course of 2014 and 2015, is a reflection of the failure of the international community, including NATO and the UN, to provide sufficient, sustained support to the state-building process following Gaddafi's ouster.[6] It is also a testament to the depth of the social divides that developed and were exacerbated over the course of Gaddafi's long rule. Redressing these lacunae will undoubtedly require more robust international engagement, including in terms of judicial and security-sector reform. This is a tall order as conflicts rage across the region and one that this book cannot address in detail. However, it must be stressed that humanitarian response alone will be insufficient to address the needs of hundreds of thousands of displaced Libyans for security and durable solutions to their predicament. Moving forward, national and international security forces working in Libya must be equipped (building on past training and capacity-building efforts) with a clear understanding of the dynamics and complexities of displacement and the strategic importance of resolving displacement crises, including through the targeted contributions of peace and security actors.[7]

Participation in Dialogues and Negotiations

Building security in Libya, and in turn resolving the internal and cross-border displacement situation, depends on a negotiated resolution to the civil war and the establishment of a unified government in Libya. While progress has reportedly been made in UN-sponsored talks in Morocco, whether this translates into a viable agreement that has traction with armed forces on the ground remains to be seen.[8] The extent to which negotiations address the rights and needs of the displaced is also an open question. National dialogue meetings in Morocco, as well as in Geneva and Ghadamis, added the question of Libyan IDPs and exiles to the agenda following constant demands from representatives of areas with IDPs. The extent to which the national dialogue will effectively address the displacement question and provide tangible solutions to it is debatable, especially considering that no representatives of the displaced community are currently taking part in ongoing dialogues.

It should be mentioned, however, that efforts to deal with the displacement question have continued on a very modest scale and at substate levels. For example, representatives of Tawergha and Misrata have met regarding reconciliation and prisoner exchanges, but this was on a small scale and did not yield major breakthroughs in the Tawerghan IDPs' situation. In January 2015, IDPs from the town of Tawergha sent representatives to the peace talks in Geneva to promote the cause of their people and push for solutions. In this instance, the hard work of the Tawerghan representatives yielded some outcomes, and several agreements were reached with Misrata, especially on the release of prisoners. The larger issue of displacement was not resolved, but the promotion of understanding between the communities and the release of some prisoners was achieved. This suggests that it would be productive for the displaced communities inside and outside Libya to have larger, more structured roles in negotiations and national dialogues.

Indeed, no one can represent the displaced communities in any future discussions of solutions better than the displaced themselves. Ensuring representation of the displaced in present and future negotiations and dialogues may improve the likelihood of successful implementation of any agreement reached about their future. As is the case in many conflicts, reaching an agreement is one thing, but implementation is an entirely different matter. The negotiating parties should not risk reaching agreements that will be resisted by the displaced communities who represent an important and populous segment of Libyan society. UN envoy Bernardino León has made impressive progress in bringing the warring parties to the negotiating table, but international mediators and warring Libyan factions themselves are generally unaware of the particular, complex concerns and challenges facing Libyan IDPs and exiles. This makes it even more necessary for displaced communities to be able to participate directly in the negotiation-and-dialogue processes so that they can communicate their concerns and ensure satisfactory solutions.[9]

Transitional Justice, Reconciliation, and the Resolution of Displacement

The security challenges facing Libya are not simply a matter of physical violence, but also economic insecurity and the absence of trust and adherence to shared norms and values.[10] This points to the need for a revamped transitional justice and reconciliation process that includes recalibrated efforts at justice-sensitive security-sector reform to remove the barriers to return and reintegration posed by overly punitive frameworks (such as the now-revoked Political Isolation Law) and dysfunctional courts.

To its credit, at different points the Libyan government has in some quarters recognized the need to engage displaced populations in transitional justice and reconciliation processes and to use these processes to advance the resolution of the country's displacement situation. For example, the fifteen-month work plan prepared for the Ministry of Justice under former justice minister al-Marghani for December 2012 to February 2014, aimed to make Libya a "state of law, justice and respect for human rights" and, more specifically, to develop "procedures related to national reconciliation in order to ease the return of internally displaced and refugees [from] abroad."[11] While government officials did make some efforts to establish committees to reach out to Libyans in the diaspora, meet with them, and identify ways to assist them, these initiatives were of limited scope and do not appear to have been sustained.[12]

Given the immense challenges the country faces, drawing attention to questions of displacement and transitional justice can be difficult. Government officials interested in promoting an even-handed, nonvindictive approach to the displacement situation face a catch-22: In order to draw sufficient attention to the situation and prompt a concerted response, it may be tempting to highlight the potential political and economic problems that could be generated by disaffected exiles—and yet this feeds into the assumptions and grievances surrounding this group that hinder willingness to engage in dialogue and consider reconciliation. While certain actors within and outside the Libyan government may wish to sustain the disenfranchisement of hardcore Gaddafi loyalists, it is important to recognize the diversity of opinions embraced by members of the diaspora, take steps to regularize relations with them, and engage them in dialogue and reconciliation processes related to the country's future.

In the absence of effective, unified government leadership in instigating dialogues with Libyans in the diaspora, various prominent Libyans have broken the taboo by reaching out to members of the former regime who have sought shelter abroad. For example, in Cairo in May 2012, the prominent Libyan religious leader Sheikh Ali Salabi met with Ahmed Qaddaf el-Damm, one of Gaddafi's cousins, in the context of an effort to identify opportunities for advancing reconciliation. Dr. Fatima Hamroush, a former minister of health in the post-Gaddafi government, has also played a leading role in convening dialogues with Libyans in the diaspora. She was able to successfully hold the first dialogue conference with Libyan opposition members in exile in Malta in March 2014. However, such initiatives are typically scattergun and must contend with vociferous opposition from the Libyan public, political parties, and media.[13] In the future, a negotiated, sustainable peace process must involve the development and implementation of a more tailored transitional justice law that purposefully seeks to relieve the retributive displacement of whole communities.[14] A carefully tailored approach to the country's complex property-restitution cases will also be needed—a challenge that is largely outside the scope of this analysis but has been addressed in detail elsewhere.[15]

In the absence of a nuanced and effectively applied legal framework, some displacement-affected communities have engaged in informal negotiations between tribal leaders, with a view to identifying mutually acceptable parameters for the resolution of displacement and related grievances. Such customary approaches should be integrated into the legal framework, but at the same time their limitations must be recognized, particularly in terms of the very modest capacity of tribal sheikhs to enforce agreements and ensure that militia members do not assault returnees.[16]

Notes

1. IDMC, "Libya: State Collapse," 1.
2. Libyan reconciliation activist, interview; coordinator, Office of Displaced People's Affairs, interview.
3. Azzouz, interview.
4. Gaddafi loyalist (2), interview.
5. Gaddafi loyalist (1), interview.
6. See, for example, Chivvis, *Toppling Qaddafi*.
7. See, for example, Elizabeth Ferris, "Security Sector Reform and Ending Displacement: Important, but Neglected, Connections," Up Front (blog), September 17, 2014, http://www.brookings.edu/blogs/up-front/posts/2014/09/17-durable-solutions-displacement-peacebuilding-ferris, and William G. O'Neill, *Police Reform in Situations of Forced Displacement: Chad, Eastern Zaire, and Kosovo*, Case Studies on Transitional Justice and Displacement (Washington, DC: ICTJ/Brookings, 2012), http://www.brookings.edu/~/media/Projects/idp/tj%20case%20studies/ONeill%20Police%20Reform.pdf. Past training activities have been undertaken by actors including the United Nations Development Programme, IOM, and Mercy Corps. For overviews of training activities related to human rights and displacement conducted before the withdrawal of most international actors owing to the escalation of violence in 2014, see, for example, the annual report of the United Nations High Commissioner for Human Rights to the Twenty-Fifth Session of the Human Rights Council, January 13, 2014.
8. See, for example, "UN Says Libya Peace Talks 'Very Close' to Final Accord," Al Jazeera, April 19, 2015, http://www.aljazeera.com/news/2015/04/libya-peace-talks-close-final-accord-150419144739046.html, and "UN Envoy says Libya Latest Peace Talks Have Gone 'Well Beyond What We Have Expected," UN News Centre, March 27, 2015, http://www.un.org/apps/news/story.asp?NewsID=50438#.VV-QYk3bLmI.
9. On the complex roles of displaced populations in peace processes and negotiations, see, for example, Public International Law and Policy Group, *Peace Agreement Drafters' Handbook* (Washington, DC: Public International Law and Policy Group, 2005); James Milner, "Refugees and the Regional Dynamics of Peacebuilding," *Refugee Survey Quarterly* 28, no. 1 (2009): 13–30; and Khalid Koser, *Addressing Internal Displacement in Peace Processes, Peace Agreements and Peace-building* (Washington, DC: Brookings–Bern Project on Internal Displacement, 2007).
10. Coordinator, Office of Displaced People's Affairs, interview.
11. Libyan Ministry of Justice 15 Month Plan, quoted in ILAC, *Rule of Law Assessment Report*, 55.
12. Coordinator, Office of Displaced People's Affairs, interview.
13. Sharqieh, *Reconstructing Libya*, 6.
14. Ibid., 21.
15. See Williams, *Housing, Land and Property Issues*.
16. Sharqieh, *Reconstructing Libya*, 21.

Conclusions and Recommendations

THE CHAOS ENGULFING LIBYA, particularly since mid-2014, leaves little room for optimism that the country's internal and cross-border displacement situations will be resolved anytime soon. The following recommendations to support the management and eventual resolution of these displacement crises build on previous locally, nationally, and internationally supported efforts. In offering the following recommendations, we are cognizant of the deeply fractured nature of the Libyan government and the paramount need to restore security and address deep-rooted social divisions in order to put an end to the repeated uprooting of Libya's citizens. Indeed, establishing a unity government, improving security, and building rule of law stand out as top priorities moving forward.

Shorter-Term Recommendations

- Neighboring countries such as Tunisia have been remarkably hospitable in providing temporary shelter to hundreds of thousands of Libyans fleeing the tumult in their own country. Given the pressures hosting such a large number of exiles has placed on state services and local communities, support is needed to ensure that these countries keep their borders open and continue to respect international norms on nonrefoulement. Prompt and concerted international support for host governments should be provided, particularly through UNHCR.

- To date, the vast majority of exiled Libyans have not sought formal refugee status but have been living under the radar on expired visas in neighboring countries. This limbo situation exacts a significant socioeconomic and psychological toll for the displaced, who fear that a change in policy may result in their summary return to violence in Libya. In order to ensure that the Libyan exile population does not become irrevocably marginalized or aggrieved, gradual but concerted steps should be taken by the host governments, in cooperation with the Libyan government and international organizations such as UNHCR, to recognize and regularize the status of this population, including through the recognition of refugee status where relevant. This will require sensitive outreach and data-collection processes with members of the exile community and the careful registration and adjudication of asylum claims to ensure that those suspected of involvement in major human rights abuses are dealt with appropriately under the relevant provisions of international human rights and refugee law. UNHCR should provide continued and updated guidance to support this process.
- Libyan state actors should support and begin to rebuild ties with the internally and externally displaced population, including by responding to the socioeconomic needs and rights of the displaced. Relevant steps include resuming the payment of salaries and entitlements for qualifying displaced individuals and waiving the requirement that Libyans return to the country in order to have a new passport issued. The Libyan government should also identify avenues to provide support for access to health services and education for Libyans in Tunisia, where service systems are under considerable pressure. Immediate steps are needed to ensure that humanitarian actors in Libya have the financial and human resources required to provide emergency assistance and longer-term recovery support to IDPs.
- Increased financial support and training opportunities are needed for Libyan civil society organizations and government agencies that are on the front lines of the response to internal displacement, building on past efforts undertaken before the withdrawal of international actors in 2014.
- Increased support is needed to expand the capacity of UNSMIL to engage in the institution-building and security sector reform efforts needed in order to enable durable solutions. Displacement specialists

should be more extensively deployed as part of the UNSMIL team in order to ensure that the mission can effectively respond to Libya's complex internal and cross-border displacement situations and, in due course, ensure appropriate support is available to returnees.
- The Libyan government, host country governments, and international actors such as UNHCR and IOM should strengthen coordination mechanisms to discuss protection strategies and solutions, exchange information, and collaborate on implementation of support for durable solutions. Targeted strategies should be developed and implemented to address the immediate protection and assistance concerns facing populations who lack adequate socioeconomic resources, including housing, and to address the risk of exploitation faced by exiles.
- In cooperation with Libyan civil society organizations committed to human rights, public-awareness campaigns should be developed with a view to increasing understanding within Libyan society of the problems facing fellow citizens who are internally displaced and in exile. Given the antipathy toward the displaced that persists in many Libyan communities, improved public awareness and respect is needed to make durable solutions attainable.
- Broad, representative, and participatory national dialogues on the country's future and the negotiation of past injustices should involve the active engagement and equitable representation of the displaced community. Despite the difficulties inherent in such an endeavor, it is essential to bring the different parties who were victimized by the Gaddafi regime and more recent violence into dialogue with one another in order to chart a peaceful path toward stabilizing the country.

Longer-Term Recommendations
(Relevant for a Postconflict Context)

- Recognizing the need to engage refugees and IDPs in transitional justice and reconciliation processes and to ensure that these processes recognize and respond to arbitrary displacement as a violation in its own right, Libya's current transitional justice frameworks will, at the appropriate point, need to be revisited and revised, drawing on support from the UN Special Rapporteur on the promotion of truth, justice, reparations, and guarantees of nonrecurrence and the UN Special Rapporteur on the human rights of internally displaced persons.

- International support should be provided for the development of a policy framework and practical systems to manage the complex question of the resolution of outstanding property claims.
- The Libyan state must recognize the right of all Libyans who are abroad to voluntarily return in safety and dignity to the country and to their homes. Equally, the right of IDPs to return to their homes must also be acknowledged. Libyan citizens' right of return should be codified in national law, building on the relevant international human rights principles. In due course, the Libyan state, in cooperation with displaced communities and international partners, should identify the particular steps needed in different cases to enable displaced Libyans to exercise their right of return. For those Libyans who freely choose not to exercise their right of return, support for other durable solutions should be explored.

About the Authors

Megan Bradley is assistant professor of political science and international development studies at McGill University and a nonresident fellow with the Brookings Institution in Washington, DC. She is the author of *Refugee Repatriation: Justice, Responsibility and Redress* (Cambridge University Press, 2013) and the editor of *Forced Migration, Reconciliation and Justice* (McGill–Queen's University Press, 2015). She holds a doctorate in international relations from the University of Oxford and has worked with UNHCR, the Canadian Department of Foreign Affairs, Trade, and Development, and the International Development Research Centre.

Ibrahim Fraihat (also known as Ibrahim Sharqieh) is a senior fellow in foreign policy at the Brookings Institution's Doha Center and an adjunct professor at Georgetown University. He previously taught international conflict resolution at George Washington University and George Mason University. His research focuses on conflict resolution and post-conflict reconstruction in the Arab world, with a particular emphasis on conflict management and mediation, transitions, national reconciliation, national dialogue, and institutional reform. He has published extensively on Middle East politics, with articles appearing in *Foreign Affairs, Foreign Policy,* the *New York Times,* the *Los Angeles Times,* the *Financial Times,* and the *Christian Science Monitor,* on the CNN and Al Jazeera websites, and elsewhere. He is the author of the book *Unfinished Revolutions: Yemen, Libya, and Tunisia after the Arab Spring* (Yale University Press, 2016, http://yalepress.yale

.edu/yupbooks/book.asp?isbn=9780300215632). Professor Fraihat received a master's in international studies from Birzeit University in Palestine in 1998 and a PhD in conflict analysis and resolution from George Mason University in 2006. He is the recipient of George Mason University's Distinguished Alumni Award (2014) for his achievements in the field of conflict resolution. Dr. Fraihat can be reached at fraihat.writer@gmail.com, on Twitter @i_fraihat, and on Facebook.

Houda Mzioudet is a Tunisian journalist, commentator, and researcher on Libyan and Tunisian affairs. Since 2013, she has carried out research for the Libyan think tank the Sadeq Institute and the Brookings Doha Center. She has contributed to several media outlets, including Tunisia Live, the *Libya Herald*, Al Jazeera English, the Thomson Reuters Foundation, the BBC, and Radio Canada. She has been a guest speaker at the Brookings Doha Center, the World Social Forum Tunis 2015, the German Fulbright Association, the Project on Middle East Democracy, and elsewhere. She earned her MA in cultural studies from the University of Manouba in Tunis, Tunisia, in 2005. Mzioudet is the recipient of awards that include the British Council Foreign Language Teaching Assistantship, the Fulbright Foreign Language Teaching Assistantship, and the International Visitor Leadership Program in Conflict Sensitive Reporting Award from the US Department of State and the UN Educational, Scientific, and Cultural Organization. She also supervises American students undertaking dissertations on global cultures in Tunisia through the US-based School of International Training.

www.ingramcontent.com/pod-product-compliance
Lightning Source LLC
Chambersburg PA
CBHW051349040426
42453CB00007B/481